ROTIS AND NAANS OF INDIA
WITH ACCOMPANIMENTS

"We at Femina have published the work of Mrs. Purobi Babbar several times. Undoubtedly she is a very outstanding cookery expert and a thorough professional. I am sure her book will be of immense help to all those who are interested in the cuisine of India."

— VIMLA PATIL
Editor, Femina

September 18, 1987

ROTIS AND NAANS OF INDIA

WITH ACCOMPANIMENTS

Traditional and exotic recipes of Rotis, Vegetarian and Non-vegetarian dishes

PUROBI BABBAR

VAKILS, FEFFER AND SIMONS LTD.
Hague Building, 9, Sprott Road, Ballard Estate
Mumbai 400 001

First printing 1988
Second printing 1990
Third printing 1992
Fourth printing 1994
Fifth printing 1997
Sixth printing 2000

Price Rs. 150/-

ISBN 81-87111-20-8

Published by Mrs. Jean Trindade for Vakils, Feffer and Simons Ltd., Hague Building,
9, Sprott Road, Ballard Estate, Mumbai 400 001.

Printed by Arun K. Mehta at Vakil & Sons Ltd., Industry Manor, 2nd Floor,
Appasaheb Marathe Marg, Worli, Mumbai 400 025.

Designed by Purobi Babbar and Ayesha Shaikh

Photographs by Taiyab Badshah

Contents

Dals

Hariyali

Introduction

India is a land of infinite variety of its weather, its scenery, its people. Their languages and food are so varied that knowing this country becomes a very interesting subject. Each part of India has something of its own to offer.

Culinary art of India differs from place to place but the staple food is the "Roti" (bread). In this book, I have prepared a collection of rotis and naans being eaten in India over the years. Since I always had numerous opportunities to travel widely all over India as well as abroad, I spent a great amount of time writing travel log, studying and observing food and culture of the people, wherever I went.

The basic knowledge of nutrition rules and technique of cooking was taught to me by my mother. I have written this book bearing the fact in my mind that the recipes of this book have to be useful to every housewife of India and abroad. And also for many people who are new to cooking, and yet want to produce interesting and nutritious meals with minimum expense and time. Moreover ever-growing prices have been a perpetual villain in family budgets.

The ingredients used for the recipes in this book are available in every household kitchen of India and all the Indian grocery stores abroad. Basic ingredients for rotis and naans is aata (whole wheat flour) and maida (plain all purpose flour), makkai-ka-aata (maize flour), owar (barley flour), spices and vegetables. In order that the book is exciting as well as instructive, I have included choice and colourful recipes in it.

Good food plays a very important part in good health and a well-fed family is likely to be a happy one. Personally I agree with the saying, "Health is Wealth".

Fortunately good food does not necessarily mean expensive food. You will find in a number of recipes I have used inexpensive ingredients and most recipes (of rotis and naans) can be a meal in itself. This is not only economical but also time and energy saving.

Making and serving different kinds of rotis and naans is not only a pleasure but it is also a science and matter of skill and technique, requiring practice and no successful cook will ignore the basic rules. My recipes are carefully and scientifically worked out with skilfully balanced measures of ingredients which will give you an exact and excellent result.

Planning and serving a meal with Indian bread need not make undue demand on your time as you are free to make up a delectable menu from as few as three dishes. More dishes can be added if you wish. All you need is a little imagination and commonsense in complementing dishes as well as their flavours.

A vegetarian Indian meal generally consists of a main dish — bread, vegetable dish, pulse dish, pickle, chutney, with salad and raitas as accompaniments. Indian Sherbets and drinks are rich in vitamins unlike carbonated drinks. Sweet dishes are seldom served at the end of the meal nowadays except on Sunday, special and festive occasions. So, it is not included in the serving suggestions. But, remember not to serve a rich sweet dish after a heavy spicy meal, a lighter and chilled one will be more appreciated. Within this framework try to see the dishes you serve vary in colour, texture and flavour. For example, if the vegetable you are serving is very soft such as spinach, make sure to serve a crunchy salad with it. Serve a dry vegetable dish with a gravy dish of pulse.

However, always serve yoghurt in some form with a vegetarian meal. It is extremely wise to make a habit of serving fresh fruits (any) at the end of a meal to maintain good family health, as fresh fruits and salad purify (remove the toxins) blood and contain fair amount of roughage.

The first and only rule of roti making is follow the recipe, and that means in every detail regarding exact weight and temperature. Those of you who do not like hot food should just leave out all the chillies in my recipes. Your food will still be authentically Indian, superb in flavour and not at all hot.

I hope you will enjoy using this book and that you will find your family and friends relish your cooking.

— PUROBI BABBAR

Preface

'Roti' the most basic food of India is a fascinating subject. All over India, Roti and Naan are made from same basic ingredients — grains, salt and water, yet they have tremendous individuality. Roti, in fact, became a generic name for bread in India. With more than a thousand years of blending foreign culture with its own, India has developed a unique range of 'Rotis' made of whole wheat flour. These are called by distinctive names such as 'Chapati', 'Phulka', 'Paratha' or 'Puri' etc. Rotis made of other kind of grains have descriptive names only, thus we have 'Makkai-ki-Roti', 'Jowar-ki-Roti' (barley flour roti), 'Bajre-ki-Roti' (bajra is a grain only grown in India), 'Chawal-ki-Roti' (roti of rice flour). These Rotis have regional popularity. Rotis are popular in all parts of the country except southern and north-eastern states.

In north and central India wheat is the most commonly used grain and ground whole wheat flour called 'Aata' is the basic ingredient in most of the rotis.

The most popular roti in India is called **Chapati** which is eaten for breakfast, lunch or dinner. **Parathas** are also made from aata but are rich and flaky, because they have been spread with ghee and folded in a special way so that they are somewhat like flaky pastry. They are shallow fried on a 'tava' (griddle) with ghee (clarified butter), and more melted ghee is drizzled on top and sides of them as they cook. **Puris** are small and are deep fried so they puff like balloons. These are all unleavened.

There is a layered Roti known as **Lachhadar Paratha.** The dough is first made into a rope, then made into a circle and rolled out three times, half cooked and re-rolled and ghee is applied in between every layer while rolling. Parathas are often stuffed with mashed potatoes, minced meat, cauliflower. There is a type of paratha called **Birahi** which uses a stuffing of 'besan' (gram flour) and has an unusual taste and texture. There is another paratha called **Bathuway-ki-Roti**. Spinach or bathuway is knead together with flour. It is dark green in colour. Egg stuffed rotis are called **Baida Roti**. Roti made of 'besan' (gram flour) known as **Besan-ki-Roti** has chopped onions, garlic and tomatoes added to the dough.

A larger variety of unleavened breads can be seen in Gujarat and Rajasthan areas. Most popular is **Rotlee** made of whole wheat flour like chapati but much lighter and thinner. Same way **Dal-Dhokli, Khaman** and **Khakhra** are served in place of roti in Gujarat. I still remember whenever dal-dhokli was served in our hostels (while I was in University), no rotlee or rice was served. **Dal-Dhokli** is a complete meal in itself. Wheat flour dough is thinly rolled and cut into 2″ × 2″ pieces and cooked in a spicy lentil gravy. **Khakhras** are dry crispy rotis which remain fresh for many days. It is knead with milk and water. Another roti of Gujarat is **Bhakhri** made from bajra flour. Knead with salt and water and cooked on a dry tava (griddle), they are highly nutritious. Every 100 gms (4 oz) bajra flour contains (in gms) protein — 11.6, fat 5.0, minerals 2.3, carbohydrates 67.5, vitamin A, value I.U. (in mg) 0.33, calorie value 361.

Traditional unique breads of Rajasthan are **Baffla, Phefre, Tikkar** and **Baati** made from whole wheat flour. For **Baati** the dough is shaped into rounds and then dry roasted in an oven (but traditionally cooked in hot charcoal fire or a fire of dry cow dung). When cooked they are cleaned, cracked slightly and put into a bowl filled with ghee. **Bafflas** are cooked first in lentil soup, then dry roasted. **Phefres** are round. A thick piece of dough is lightly flattened, dry roasted first in a tava (griddle) and then put in the charcoal fire. Served with ghee and dal.

Tikkars are very popular among the peasants of Rajasthan. This is a thick roti made of wheat and corn flour, mixed with lot of chopped garlic, onion, tomatoes, green chillies and coriander leaves. Very little oil is used and it is cooked almost dry in a tava (griddle). **Dopattri** rotis are also very popular in Malwa area. They are soft and thin chapatis like rotis. But when pulled part, two separate rotis can be seen. The secret of this roti is the technique of rolling the dough. Same way the popular roti among peasants of Marwar (Rajasthan) is **Batia**.

Then there are those breads that do have leavening and therefore take longer to make such as **Naan**. The naan is a Persian word which means bread. Exactly as does the Indian word Roti. The main differences between the two is in the flour and cooking method. Names of the breads baked in 'Tandoor' provide further evidence of their origin. There are also many elaborated naans. The first step above the plain one is the **Roghni Naan**. The name means red naan because before baking, the naan is given brushing of saffron water. Then there is the **Khurmee Naan**. Originally this naan was coated with a mixture of khurma (dates) and gur (jaggery) cooked together. Also there is tomato and garlic naan. Coated with tomato sauce and garlic paste. **Badami Naan, Paneer Naan, Taftan** are the names given to a delicious variety of naans made with milk, eggs and yoghurt. The range of naans available in India is so varied and so delicious that one could eat them by itself with dahi (yoghurt), chutneys or achaars (pickles).

The **Kulcha** is another import from Western Asia. It is made from maida (plain all purpose flour). But it is different from naan in many ways (in its original form). The **Kulcha** is knead with much more ghee than in the naan. The kulchas are round in shape and can be stuffed with a variety of fillings like parathas and puris. Another mouth watering roti (bread) called **Sheer-Maal** also has Persian influence. 'Sheer' in Persian means milk. Then comes **Baquarkhani,** a naan which is an elaborate variation of Sheer-Maal except that it is fried on a griddle rather than baked in a tandoor.

Another delicious roti made in the tandoor is **Khasta Roti** (popular among northern India) which is crisp because it is enriched with butter and then baked in a tandoor. It tastes like a pie crust. The naan on the other hand is much softer.

I was astonished to see the striking similarities between Indian **Makkai-ki-Roti** and the Mexican **Tortilla.** Only difference is that tortilla is covered and decorated with fried eggs, cheese and tomato slices and sliced ham or also served plain with some other dish whilst makkai-ki-roti is served plain with saag or dahi.

The bread in Tashkent (in Soviet Central Asia) is almost identical to the morning bread of Kashmir (round loaves with an indentation in the centre bearing a distinctive pattern formed by an intersecting line). The same similarities are present between **Naan** and the bread of Midddle East. Both are leavened, flat and made of plain white flour. **Pittas** are round and **Naans** are tear-drop shape. Another counterpart of Sindhi **'Pakwan'** I have found in Wien (Vienna) and I ate it to make sure. It was plain (in pakwan sometimes, salt and ajwain (curum) are used) and fried before it is served. Indian **Rumali Roti** also is a first cousin of the **Sharak** bread of Bedouins.

They are so similar as to make one wonder how the similarity came about. Both are very thin and as large as a bicycle wheel and both are cooked on a convex griddle (ultra tava). The name of this roti means it is as thin as a silken scarf. It is a truly fine bread, which is not rolled to achieve its thinness. These rumali roti makers reminds you of those nimble fingered hawkers who make 'Murataba' (called Murtaback after it is stuffed) in Singapore and Malaysia.

Today the most popular and distinctive bread of Bombay is **Pao** (eaten with bhaji) or **Double Roti** which is similar in taste to the sandwich bread. Yet another import from Western Asia is the **Muslim Naan** (a leavened bread) and is only available in Bombay and Surat, among Muslim residential localities. After the disc is baked and brushed with oil, the naan is cut into six or eight portions in the form of segments and eaten with mughlai chicken or meat. Roadside vendors serve smaller versions of these naans with a delicious minced meat cooked with oil. The minced meat is placed over low heat with a lot of green chillies and is allowed to simmer for 5 to 6 hours. It is called 'Naan-Chap'.

The **Yehudi Roti** or Jewish roti came to India with the Jews of Baghdad. It is made of plain (all purpose flour) maida mixed with the khameer and knead with water. It is rolled out into a thin round disc like chapati or roti, but the traditional method of making this roti is slightly different. The flattened circular dough is placed on a larger round cushion and stretched out to cover the diameter of the cushion then the cushion is swung into the tandoor. The cushion is then removed and the rotis, when done, are peeled out with tongs and served with grilled meat. Although Baghdadi Jews have migrated to Israel, but their bakeries in central Bombay area still continue to make this roti exactly the same way.

Andey-ki-Roti is another delicious variety of bread, which is only available in Bombay. It is a meal in itself made with eggs, minced green chillies, mint and coriander leaves. This roti does not require any accompaniments.

Those who live in Calcutta are very familiar with **Kathi Rolls** of Nizams (behind New Market) which make an excellent quick meal. It is a feather soft, stuffed roti, made from plain flour (maida). After the roti is cooked, stuffing is placed in the centre and the roti is rolled like a swiss roll and wrapped half way with butter paper. Eggs, meat or chicken are used for stuffing. **Kathi Rolls, Dhakai Paratha, Radha Bollobhi Luchi** are the pride of Calcutta like **Andey-ki-Roti** is of Bombay.

The culinary offerings of southern India are different again. The coconut plays a commanding role, and rice flour largely replaces wheat. There are over ten different types of **Dosai** available all over southern India. I have included a few in this book. Some varieties of Dosai are now prepared only in the villages and smaller towns of South India. But still you can taste those rare varieties of Dosai in Madras and Coimbatore called **Rocket Dosai** or **Family Dosai** over 5 ft. diameter. It requires two waiters to place it on the table. Another unique Dosai is **Set Dosai** in which two pale yellowish Dosai are sandwiched with a vegetable curry.

All the recipes of this book are tried in our kitchen several times till I achieved the correct measurements of ingredients. And I can assure my readers that if the instructions are carefully followed the results will be satisfying.

I cannot sufficiently express my gratitude to my husband for the moral support he has always rendered to me.

I would like to also express my appreciation and gratitude to my publisher, Mrs. Ayesha Shaikh for her sincere help and hard work.

I sincerely thank Mr. & Mrs. Sunil Mehta, Mrs. Jean Trindade, Mr. D. Tavre and his staff of Taj Mahal Hotel, Bombay and Miss Asha Pehlajani for their help.

— PUROBI BABBAR
INDORE, INDIA

Weights, Measures and Temperatures

All recipes in this book are based on Imperial and Metric weights and measures. These tables are provided as a guide. It is important to remember the following points:

(a) The **exact** conversions from Imperial to Metric frequently give inconvenient working quantities. Therefore the ounce is converted to 25 grams.

(b) When using the 25 gm unit for one ounce you will find size of the cooked dish will be slightly smaller.

Conversion Tables

These are approximate conversions, which have been rounded up or down. Do not mix metric and imperial measures in one recipe.

Weight

Imperial ounces	Proximate grams to the nearest whole figure	Recommended conversion to the nearest unit of 25 gm
1	28	25
2	57	50
3	85	75
4	113	100
5	142	150
6	170	175
7	198	200
8 (½ lb)	226	225
16 (1 lb)	456	450
32 (2 lb)	907	900
35 (2 lb 3 oz)	997	1 Kilogram

Measures in weight in the Imperial and American system are the same, only measures in volume are different. Following tables show the equivalents.

Metric	Imperial	American
5 ml	1 tsp	1 tsp
15 ml	1 tbsp	1 tbsp
30 ml	2 tbsps	3 tbsps
	3½ tbsps	4 tbsps
	4 tbsps	5 tbsps

Liquid Measure

Imperial fluid ounce	Exact conversion	Working equivalent
¼ pint (1 gill)	142 milli litre	150 ml
½ pint	284 ml	300 ml
1 pint	568 ml	600 ml
1¾ pint	994 ml	1 litre

Spoon measures — level spoon measurements are used throughout the book

Tea Cups:

The average Indian tea cup is about 210 ml (7 fl oz). Corresponding adjustments should be made if using larger or smaller cups.

A British standard cup is 275 ml (10 fl oz). But an American or Canadian standard cup is 8 fl oz.

Metric, Imperial and American cup measures are given in this book, so you can use whichever you prefer. But use only one or the other — the amounts are not always interchangeable.

Oven Temperatures: The temperatures in the recipes are according to this chart. But it would be best to refer to your oven's temperature chart as different makes of ovens vary.

	°C.	°F.	Gas Mark
Very Cool	110°	225°	¼
	120°	250°	½
Cool	140°	275°	1
	150°	300°	2
Warm	160°	325°	3
Moderate	180°	350°	4
Moderate Hot	190°	375°	5
Fairly Hot	200°	400°	6
Hot	220°	425°	7
Very Hot	230°	450°	8
	240°	475°	9

How to make at home

Paneer or Chana

Heat 1 litre milk, bring it to a boil stirring continuously to prevent the cream forming on the top.
Remove from heat and add 2 tbsps lime juice.
Stir till the milk curdles and let it stand for 20 minutes.
Strain through a muslin cloth and squeeze out all the liquid. The cream cheese thus formed is called paneer or chana. Put a weight over the paneer for 30 minutes.

Coconut Milk

Mix 2 cups of grated coconut with 2 cups of hot water.
Leave it to cool, then squeeze out the milk.
If fresh coconut is not available, use packed flaked preserved coconut and squeeze out the milk.

Saffron Water

Soak ½ tsp. of saffron with 2 tbsps hot water. When cooled, mix well and use the coloured water.

Khoya

Boil 1 litre milk over high heat until it becomes thick and all water in milk dries up. This solid milk is called khoya or mawa.

Quick Khoya

To 1 cup instant full cream milk powder add 2 tbsps water. Mix to a stiff consistency. Makes approximately 125 gms khoya.

Khameer

Take 4 oz (100 gms) maida (all purpose plain flour), ½ tsp of sugar, 1 level tsp of salt, 6 oz (175 gms) yoghurt (dahi). Mix these together into a thin batter. This should be kept in a warm place. It will ferment overnight and turn into the leavening called 'Khameer'.

Pressed Paneer (Cottage Cheese)

Flatten the paneer immediately after it is made. Wrap the paneer with a piece of clean muslin. Place on a plate. Flatten to 1" thickness by placing a weight over it for 4-5 hours. Remove the cloth carefully and cut into required shapes.

Zeera Paneer

Add 2 tbsps ground roasted cumin seeds to the milk after adding lemon juice. Tie and flatten by placing a weight over it for 4-6 hours. Cut into cubes. Squeeze some lemon juice over the pieces and serve as an appetizer.

Basic Tomato Sauce

Cooking time: 45 minutes   Makes: 2½ cups

500 gms ripe tomatoes, washed and sliced
100 gms onion, chopped
225 gms cooking apples (optional)

5/8 cup vinegar — (½ cup + 2 tbsps)
1 tsp salt
100 gms sugar
7 cloves

10 peppercorns, 1″ piece of ginger, crushed, 2 dry red chillies — tied up in a piece of muslin

Place tomatoes, onion, apples (if used) in a pan. Cover and cook gently over low heat until softened.
Add sugar, salt and vinegar and spices tied in a piece of muslin. Simmer gently for 30 minutes.
Sieve the mixture. And simmer again for 15 minutes uncovered. Stir constantly.
Pour into a hot jar. Seal carefully and sterilize.

Note: If apple is used the colour will be little brown.

Vegetarian Kheema

Boil 4 oz (100 gms) Nutri Nuggets, wash several times and mince finely.

Chaat Masala

3 tsps roasted cumin seeds
2 tsps black salt
1 tsp dry ginger

¼ tsp asafoetida
1 tsp red chilli powder
1 tsp black pepper

5 tsps dried mango powder
2 tsps white salt

Pound and powder all the ingredients together and serve as required.

Panch Phoran

25 gms aniseeds
25 gms nigella seeds
25 gms cumin seeds

25 gms mustard seeds
25 gms fenugreek seeds

Mix all the ingredients together and keep in an airtight bottle.

Sambar Masala

0 gms dry red chillies
5 gms coriander seeds

1 tbsp fenugreek seeds
1 tbsp mustard seeds

Dry fry each spice separately for about 8-10 minutes. Fry the fenugreek and mustard seeds until they begin to pop and splutter and fenugreek seeds should turn light brown. Cool and grind them into a fine powder.
Use 1 full tbsp of the masala to make 8 cups of sambar.

Dhania Zeera

00 gms coriander seeds
5 gms cumin seeds

6 dry red chillies (remove the stalks)

Dry grind all the ingredients to a fine powder. Store in an air tight container.

Garam Masala 1

tbsps cumin seeds
tbsps coriander seeds
tbsp black peppercorns

2 tbsps cardamom seeds
4 (3") pieces of cinnamon sticks

½ nutmeg
1 tsp whole cloves

Dry roast each spice separately. Dry grind together except nutmeg. Grate nutmeg and mix in. Store in an air tight bottle.

Garam Masala 2

(3") pieces of cinnamon sticks
tsp whole cloves

2 tsps cardamom seeds
1 tsp blades of mace

Roast and dry grind.

Kashmiri Garam Masala

tsp black cumin seeds
tsps cardamom seeds

1 tsp whole peppercorns

2 (2") pieces of cinnamon
1 tsp. whole cloves
⅓ of a nutmeg, grated

Dry roast all the spices and grind to a fine powder. Add nutmeg. Store in an air tight bottle.

19

Madras Curry Masala

1 cup coriander, ground
½ cup cumin, ground
1 tbsp each chilli powder, turmeric,
mustard, black pepper and salt

8 cloves garlic, crushed
2 tbsps fresh ginger, grated
¾ cup oil
2 tbsps vinegar, for mixing

Mix the ground spices and salt in a bowl.
Add garlic, ginger and vinegar. Mix well. Make a puree.
Heat oil in a pan till smoking hot and add the spices mixture. Reduce heat. Stir constantly
until spices are cooked and oil separates from spices. Cool and bottle.

Tamarind Pulp

100 gms tamarind   1 cup hot water   A pinch of salt

Soak the tamarind in hot water for 30 minutes. Add salt. Mix well and strain.

Glossary

Flours

	Hindi Terms
Whole wheat flour	Aata
Plain white flour or all purpose flour	Maida
Barley flour	Jowar ka aata
Rice flour	Chaaval ka aata
Gram flour	Besan
Semolina	Rawa
Corn meal	Makkai ka aata
Millet flour	Bajri or Bajra ka aata

Pulses

Bengal gram	Chana dal
Chick peas	Kabuli chana
Black gram	Urad dal
Whole green gram	Sabat mung dal
Split green gram	Dhuli mung dal
Lentil (split or whole)	Masoor ki dal
Black eyed bean	Chowley or Lobia
Red gram (split)	Arhar/Tuvar dal
Kidney bean	Rajmah

Indian herbs

Coriander leaves	Hara dhania or kothmir
Basil	Tulsi
Bay leaves	Tej patta
Mint leaves	Pudina
Curry leaves	Curry patta or mitha neem
Fenugreek leaves	Hari methi
Garlic	Lasun
Fresh ginger	Adrak

Spices

Aniseeds or fennel seeds	Saunf
Asafoetida	Hing
Curum	Ajwain
Black pepper	Kali mirch
Cardamom	Chotee illaichi
Black cardamom	Kali illaichi (not to be eaten raw)

Chilli	Lal mirch
Green chilli	Hari mirch
Cinnamon	Dalchini
Cloves	Lavang
Coriander seeds	Sookha dhania
Cumin seeds	Zeera
White cumin	Safed zeera
Black cumin	Shah zeera
Fenugreek	Methi dana
Mace	Javantri
Dry ginger	Soonth
Mango powder	Aamchur
Mustard seeds	Rai or sarson
Nigella seeds	Kalonji
Poppy seeds	Khus-khus
Saffron	Zaffran or kesar
Sesame seeds	Gingelly or til
Turmeric	Haldi
Nutmeg	Jaiphal
Black salt or Rock salt	Kala namak

Nuts and Seeds

Almond	Badam
Cashewnut	Kaju
Charoli seeds	Chironji
Dry coconut	Sukha narial
Peanut or groundnut	Moong phali — singdana
Pistachio	Pista
Walnut	Akhrot
Raisin	Kishmish

Vegetables and Fruits

Artichoke	Hattichak
Ash gourd	Karela
Aubergine	Baingan
Cauliflower	Phulgobi
Cabbage	Bandh gobi
Parwar	Parwal
Green peas	Mutter
Pumpkin	Kaddu
Snake gourd	Chahehinda
Marrow	Ghia

Capsicum	Simla mirch
French bean	Farash bean
Okra or Lady finger	Bhindi
Cluster bean	Guar ki phali
Arbi	Dasheen
Cucumber	Khira
Drumstick	Suijan ki phali
Potato	Alu
Beetroot	Chukander
Radish	Muli
Turnip	Shalgam
Yam (Elephant)	Zaminkand
Yam (ordinary)	Ratalu
Sweet potato	Shakarkand
Onion	Piaz
Spinach	Palak
Carrot	Gaajar
Lettuce	Salad ka patta
Fenugreek leaves	Methi ka saag
Colocasia	Arbi ka saag

Fruits

Apple	Seb
Mango green	Keri
Mango	Aam
Jack fruit	Kathal
Banana	Kela
Apricot	Khubani
Date	Khajur
Grape	Angoor
Guava	Amrood
Indian Prune	Alubokhara
Fig	Anjeer
Water melon	Tarbooz
Papaya	Papita
Peach	Ardoo
Pear	Nashpati
Pineapple	Ananas
Plum (red)	Alubukhara
Orange	Santra or Narangi
Sweet lime	Mausambi

Goa Chillies

These chillies are grown in southern India. They have a thick skin and resemble Italian peppers in size and shape. They impart a rich red colour and flavour to curry without much pungency.

Madrasi Chillies

Shorter variety more scarlet than deep red in colour and much more pungent than Goa or Kashmiri chillies.

Tamri Bhaji

(Chawli Bhaji) Red spinach.

Kashmiri Chillies

They are longer and have rich red colour. Not so pungent and used usually for colour.

Kokum

(Binda sola). The fleshy skin of this fruit dried and stored. It must be washed and soaked before using.

Bedgi Chillies

Very pungent orange colour chillies, much more pungent than Kashmiri or Goa chillies.

Surya Mukhi

Chillies or Assam chillies — hardly 1″ to 1½″ in size. Green chillies as thick as a finger but they grow facing upwards rather than facing downwards like other variety of chillies. Quite pungent.

Kunkuni

(Naga chillies) These are very small chillies, size of a Basmati rice. Grown in a bushy tree of 4 feet facing upwards, these are extremely pungent. May be one little chilli equal to two Bedgi chillies. Eaten raw with food.

Teflan

(Chirphul)
Fresh berries are green with a black seed. Can be used raw or dried till colour turns black. It can be stored. To use — soak in water for a few minutes then crush well. Discard seeds and use only the skins for flavouring.

Cooking Terms

Bake	:	To cook by dry heat in oven or tandoor.
Batter	:	Any mixture of dry ingredients and liquid that is stirred or beaten can be poured.
Beat	:	Means quite vigorous action, generally with wooden spoon:

(a) You beat the ingredients for a batter.

(b) You beat fat and sugar in creaming.

(c) You beat a sauce as it thickens.

Blanch	:	To put food in cold or hot water in order to either whiten or remove the skin.
Blend	:	To combine ingredients thoroughly until very smooth and uniform.
Boil	:	To cook at boiling point.
Brush	:	To spread thinly with a brush.
To chop	:	To cut food into very small pieces with a sharp knife.
Consistency	:	A term describing the texture usually the thickness of a mixture.
Core	:	Remove the inner portion.
Cubes	:	Small equal pieces usually of about ½" each side.
Dice	:	To cut into small cubes, generally of about ¼" size.
Dough	:	A mixture of flour and liquid also with other ingredients, thick enough to knead and roll.
Dissolve	:	To make a solution with a liquid and a dry substance e.g. yeast and milk.
To grate	:	To rub food against the grate and a term used for variety of things, such as cheese, fruits, onions and fruit rind. While grating the rind of the fruit be very careful not to grate too deep. You take only the 'ZEST' (bright colour part) of the fruit skin.
Garnish	:	To decorate with part of colourful contrasting food.
Grill	:	Cooking quickly under red hot grill used for small tender pieces of meat, fish or browning food etc. Never try to grill tough meat or poultry and keep food well moistened with a little oil or melted fat.
Grind	:	To crush the ingredients into powder form.
Knead	:	This is the movement of incorporating the ingredients used in rotis and naans and to a lesser degree in biscuits and pastry.

Marinate	:	To soak food in liquid e.g. lemon juice, vinegar or tandoori masala to soften and flavour it.
Prove	:	Means to cause yeast dough to rise (the process is explained in the recipes) until it has increased its bulk to twice the original size by keeping in a warm place.
Simmering	:	Cooking over low heat, just below boiling point so that the liquid bubbles gently at the side of the pan.
Shred	:	Means to cut into very narrow pieces e.g. you shred almonds, cabbage etc.
Sift or sieve	:	To pass through a fine sieve so as to remove lumps.
Stock	:	The liquid in which vegetables are cooked.
Stir	:	A fairly brisk movement to mix with spoon etc. (a wooden spoon is the best thing to use) using a rotary motion.
Saute	:	Stir fry, in little oil, crispness must be maintained.

Thandai

Almond milk drink of Punjab

150 gms almonds
2 cups (425 ml) milk
10 peppercorns

3 cups (750 ml) water
1 cup (160 gms) castor sugar
4 tbsps sunflower seeds

1 tbsp rose water or essence

* Blanch almonds, put into an electric blender with half the water, sunflower seeds and peppercorns. Blend at high speed until finely ground.
* Strain through a clean muslin cloth into a jug.
* Return the ground mixture left in the cloth to the blender with remaining water. Blend again and extract the liquid once more.
* Mix milk, almond extract, sugar and stir until dissolved.
* Add rose water or essence to flavour.
* Chill. Stir well before serving. Serve with crushed ice and few small rose petals on top of the drink.

Preparation time: 15 minutes   Makes: 4 glasses

Am ka Masala Sherbet

Spicy green mango drink

medium raw mangoes
level tbsps sugar
tbsp cumin seeds, roasted and
ground

½ tsp ground pepper
1 tsp salt
1 tsp chilli powder (optional)
4 cups (1 lt) chilled water

2 tbsps basil leaves (tulsi),
finely chopped
½ tsp black salt (optional)

Place the mangoes under hot grill until done or roast directly over glowing coal or boil them.
Carefully cut the top, a small portion and squeeze out the pulp. Remove skin.
Place pulp with seeds in a bowl. Add water, salt, black salt, sugar, chilli, pepper. Mix well. Chill.
Just before serving, strain and discard seeds. Add roasted ground cumin seeds and basil leaves to the chilled sherbet.

Preparation time: 20 minutes   Makes: 5 small glasses

Zeera Pani

Cumin and tamarind drink

2½ cups (575 ml) hot water
⅝ cup (150 ml) tamarind pulp
3 tsps ginger, finely grated
2 tsps cumin seeds, roasted and ground

Pinch of chilli powder
½ tsp garam masala
3 level tsps sugar
2 level tsps salt

Mint sprig and lemon slices to garnish
Ice water and crushed ice for serving.

☆ Mix all the ingredients with hot water. Stir well.
☆ Strain through a nylon sieve. Chill.
☆ Add ice water. Pour into individual glasses. Garnish with mint leaves and lemon slices. Serve with ice.

Preparation time: 1 hour   To serve: 4

Hara Nariyal Pani

Green coconut water

2 green coconuts (put overnight in refrigerator)

2 tbsps rose water

2 tbsps basil leaves (tulsi), finely chopped

☆ Cut coconut. Pour water into a bowl. Add rose water and chopped basil.
☆ Scrape out if any malai (coconut flesh) is inside shell. Serve this separately.
☆ Pour into tall individual glasses and serve.

Preparation time: 5 minutes   To serve: 4

Aab-e-Bahar

Fresh coconut water, flavoured with honey and fresh lime

4 green coconuts	4 tbsps lime juice	Chopped mint leaves
4 tbsps honey	4 lime peel curls	

* Cut the coconuts and take out water.
* Mix all the ingredients and coconut water together. Serve in tall glasses. Decorate with lemon curls and sprinkle mint leaves.

Preparation time: 10 minutes   To serve: 4

Kanji

Punjabi black carrot drink

1 kg black carrots	2 level tbsps chilli powder	4 lts hot water
3 tbsps mustard seeds	2 level tbsps salt	A few sprigs mint leaves

* Wash and scrape the carrots, cut into four lengthwise.
* Dry grind the mustard seeds.
* Mix together carrots, salt, mustard and chilli.
* Gently add water, mix well.
* Put the mixture into a large bottle or achaar barni. Close the lid tightly.
* Put in the sun for 5-6 days. Shake the bottle few times a day.
* Chill kanji before serving. Sprinkle chopped mint and serve.

Preparation time: 5-6 days   Makes: 5 litres

29

Falooda

Ice cold milk drink with vermicelli and ice-cream

2½ cups (575 ml) cold milk
6 tbsps rose syrup or Rooh Afza
3 tsps tulsi seeds, **soaked for 4/5 hours**

4 heaped tbsps granulated sugar
3 scoops vanilla ice-cream

For falooda
1½ heaped tbsps cornflour
2 cups (425 ml) water
1¼ cups (275 ml) ice water

☆ Mix together cornflour and water and cook over low heat, stirring constantly until it begins to look transparent.
☆ Place the mixture into a colander, place it over the pan containing ice water. Now with the back of wooden spoon press the mixture through. The pieces will fall into the ice water and solidify. Keep aside for 30 minutes, then strain.
☆ Heat milk and sugar and chill.
☆ Place 2 tsps of tulsi seeds, 2 tbsps cornflour falooda, in the bottom of each glass. Add rose syrup and crushed ice. Pour in the cold milk. Place a scoop of vanilla ice-cream on top.

Note: There are many Indian summer drinks but this one is a favourite of all. It gets its name from the cornflour vermicelli that floats in it. Many people replace it with tiny pieces of jelly made of 'China Grass'. But easy substitute is 'cellophane' noodles (bean starch noodles), they are soaked and boiled until transparent, then cut into short length. Falooda can be served as a dessert.

Preparation time: 1 hour   Makes: 3 glasses

Basic Lassi (Namkin)

Indian yoghurt drink

1 cup (250 ml) plain yoghurt
2½ cups (575 ml) cold water
1 level tsp salt

1 level tsp cumin seeds, roasted and ground
1 tbsp fresh mint, finely chopped

Dash of ground black pepper
Crushed ice

☆ Put all the ingredients except the ice and mint in a food processor or blender and mix at high speed for 2 minutes.
☆ Place some crushed ice into individual glasses, pour the prepared lassi, and sprinkle chopped mint. Serve immediately.

Variations:

Mithi Lassi: Add 4 tsps of sugar to 1 cup yoghurt and 2½ cups water. Blend at high speed. Sprinkle little cardamom powder and finely shredded blanched almonds or pistachio nuts.

Santara ki Lassi: Peel one orange. Separate the segments. Take a sharp knife, cut thinly the front part of each segment. Remove seeds and white skin. Place them in a plate, break the orange segments lightly. Add it to the sweetened lassi. (Picture on page 101).

Mausambi Lassi: Same as above. Add segments to sweetened lassi.

Seb ki Lassi (Apple): Peel and grate one small apple, toss in lime juice, add it to the sweetened lassi.

Ananas ki Lassi: Finely chop pieces of pineapple. Add 2 tbsps per glass of sweetened lassi. Sprinkle chopped mint or parsley on top.

Chiku ki Lassi: Take one chiku per glass. Peel and halve. Remove seeds. Put them into a blender. Make a puree and pour equal amount into each glass then pour sweetened lassi. Stir well. Top with few grains of brown sugar.

Aam ki Lassi (Mango Lassi): Peel and chop 1 or 2 ripe Alphonso mangoes. Put into the blender, make a puree. Add 5 tbsps of puree to each glass of sweetened lassi. Top with nutmeg powder.

Angoor ki Lassi: Wash and crush 100 gms seedless grapes well. Add it to 2 cups sweetened lassi. (Picture on page 205).

Makes: 2 glasses

Papita Lassi

Papaya lassi

1 cup diced ripe papaya,
mashed well
1 cup (250 gms) plain yoghurt
2 cups chilled water

2 tbsps lime juice
1 tsp salt
½ tsp pepper

Few sprigs of mint
Ice cubes

* ☆ Make lassi. Beat yoghurt, then add water, beat again.
* ☆ Add mashed papaya with all seasoning. Beat well.
* ☆ Pour into individual glasses. Garnish with mint and serve cold.
* ☆ If you want to make sweet papaya lassi then omit salt, lime juice and pepper. Add 2 tbsps sugar instead and flavour with rose water.

Preparation time: 10 minutes   Makes: 6 glasses

Adrak ki Lassi

1 cup (250 gms) yoghurt
2 cups (425 ml) chilled water

2 tbsps fresh ginger juice *OR*
1 tsp dry ginger powder

1 dry red kashmiri chilli,
roasted and chopped
2 level tsps salt

* ☆ Make lassi and mix all other ingredients.
* ☆ Serve with crushed ice.

Preparation time: 5 minutes   Makes: 5 glasses

Facing Page
Clockwise:

Shorba-e-Masta-va-Khai
Besan ki Roti
Dhohdha
Sindhi Sai Bhaji

Punjab di Chach

Buttermilk drink of Punjab

4 cups (1 lt) buttermilk (plain, see page 31)
½ tsp fresh ginger slices
2 dry Kashmiri red chillies or chilli powder

2 level tsps salt
1 tsp mustard seeds
½ tsp mint or parsley, finely chopped

2 tsps oil
Ice cubes

* Dry roast the chilli and chop finely.
* Add chillies, salt and ginger to the buttermilk. Stir.
* Heat oil and fry mustard seeds, when it crackles pour onto the buttermilk mixture. Chill.
* Pour into individual glasses, sprinkle mint. Add ice and serve.

Preparation time: 10 minutes	Makes: 5 glasses

Angoor ka Sherbet

225 gms seedless grapes
3 tbsps castor sugar
½ tsp ground pepper

1 level tsp cumin seeds, roasted and ground
½ level tsp salt

2 tsps lemon juice
3 cups (750 ml) chilled water
Few sprigs of mint

* Wash grapes and crush them thoroughly.
* Pour in water. Mix well. Strain through a nylon sieve.
* Add all the seasoning. Mix well. Chill. Serve, garnished with mint leaves.

Preparation time: 20 minutes	Makes: 6 large glasses

Facing Page
Clockwise:

Tandoori Roti
Khasta Roti
Bhature
Sundal
Bhutte ki Sabzi

Phalon ka Sherbet

Mixed fruit drink

4 cups lemonade
Juice of 2 lemons
1 cup (160 gms) castor sugar
1 orange, peeled and chopped
1 apple, quartered with peel and thinly sliced

1 cup grapes, halved and pips removed
2 slices tinned pineapple, finely chopped
1 pear, peeled, quartered and thinly sliced

2 tsps mint leaves, chopped
Grated rind of 1 lemon
4 tsps honey
1 cup (275 ml) water
1 cup red rose petals, washed

☆ Mix water and sugar, stir well. Add lemonade and lemon juice.
☆ Add all cut fruits, lemon rind, rose petals, honey and mint. Chill.
☆ Serve with ice cubes.

Preparation time: 25 minutes	Makes: 4 large glasses

Panaa

Spicy mango drink with saffron of Maharashtra

5 semi ripe Alphonso mangoes
5 tbsps granulated sugar
½ tsp salt

10 strands of saffron, soaked with 2 tsps water
2½ cups (575 ml) chilled water

2 tsps chironji, roasted dry

☆ Spear each mango one at a time with a fork and hold over direct flame or place them under hot grill until both the sides completely scorch the skin, turning them few times. Cool and peel off all skin.
☆ Scrape the cooked pulp sticking to the peels.
☆ Put pulp, sugar, salt and saffron in a blender. Blend well.
☆ Pour into a bowl, add water and chill.
☆ Serve cold garnished with chironji.

Note: If you wish to preserve then do not add water. Put the thick juice in a bottle. Dilute with chilled water just before serving. Remains in refrigerator for a week.

Cooking time: 20 minutes	Makes: 8 glasses

Malabar Narengi Ras

Malabar style orange juice

2½ cups (575 ml) orange juice
1 level tsp salt

½ tsp roasted cumin seeds powder
1 tbsp basil or mint leaves, finely
chopped

Ice cubes

✴ Mix all ingredients together and chill. Serve in individual glasses with ice cubes.

Preparation time: 15 minutes	Makes: 3 small glasses	Picture on page: 223

Karha

Indian herbal tea

2½ cups (575 ml) water
8 basil leaves
6 peppercorns

½ tsp aniseeds
2 tbsps crushed palm sugar candy
OR plain sugar candy (mishri)

½" piece of ginger, crushed
1 tsp tea leaves or 1 bag
6 tbsps milk

✴ Heat water add basil, peppercorns, ginger, aniseeds and palm sugar. Increase heat and bring to a boil.
✴ Add tea leaves. Reduce heat, simmer 3-4 minutes and remove from heat. Add milk.
✴ Strain into individual cups and serve hot.

Note: An excellent remedy for sore throat and cold.

Cooking time: 25 minutes	Makes: 3 cups

Qahwa

Kashmiri tea

4 cups water
2 small green cardamoms, shelled
and powdered

½" piece of cinnamon, powdered
1 tsp fresh green tea
5 almonds, shredded

6 strands saffron, crushed
(optional)
Sugar to taste

★ Place water and tea leaves in a pan. Bring to boil. Strain.
★ Put in the cardamom, cinnamon, shredded almonds and saffron, and heat.
★ Pour into individual cups. Serve at once.

Cooking time: 25 minutes   Makes: 4 small cups

Shorba-e-Masta-Va-Khair

Cucumber and yoghurt soup

1 medium size cucumber, thinly sliced
1 cup (250 ml) yoghurt
2½ cups (570 ml) water or stock
1 small onion, finely chopped

1 stick cinnamon
3 shelled walnuts, finely chopped
2 tbsps raisins, soaked previously
2 tbsps finely chopped parsley

1 tbsp dried mint leaves, chopped
1½ tsps salt
1 tbsp oil

* Heat oil, fry onion until lightly browned.
* Add sliced cucumber with stock. Keep aside few slices for garnishing.
* Put yoghurt with cinnamon, mint, salt, raisins. Simmer few minutes.
* Serve hot or cold. Sprinkle chopped walnuts, parsley and place cucumber slices on top.

| Cooking time: 25 minutes | To serve: 4-6 | Picture on page: 33 |

Saar

Maharashtrian spicy broth with tomatoes and coconut

500 gms tomatoes, chopped
1 cup (250 ml) coconut milk (see page 17)
1 green chilli, seeded and chopped

2½ cups (575 ml) hot water
1 tsp cornflour
2½ level tsps salt
½ tsp pepper

4 tsps jaggery, grated
6 curry leaves
2 tbsps coriander leaves, finely chopped

* Put tomatoes into an electric blender and blend to a smooth puree. Strain and keep aside.
* Place tomato puree and water in a pan, bring to a boil. Simmer over low heat. Add salt, pepper, jaggery and chilli.
* Mix cornflour with little coconut milk. Add it to the boiling tomato puree with remaining coconut milk. Boil another 5 minutes.
* Garnish with coriander and curry leaves. Serve hot.

| Cooking time: 30 minutes | To serve: 4-6 |

Amti

Maharashtrian lentil soup with coconut

1 cup (160 gms) lentil or spilt peas
8 cups (2 lt) water
1 tbsp tamarind pulp (see page 20)
½ tsp turmeric powder
2 tsps jaggery or brown sugar

½ tsp black mustard seeds
3 green chillies, seeded and
chopped
3 cloves garlic, crushed
6 curry leaves
2 tbsps desiccated coconut

2 level tbsps salt
1 tbsp oil
2 tbsps coriander leaves,
finely chopped for garnishing

☆ Put together lentil, turmeric and half water in a pan. Bring to a boil. Cover and cook over low heat for one hour until lentil is very soft. Pour in remaining water.
☆ Add salt and tamarind pulp into the boiling lentil.
☆ Add sugar or jaggery.
☆ Heat oil in a pan. Fry the curry leaves, mustard seeds and chillies until the mustard seeds pop. Add garlic, stir and fry until golden colour.
☆ Add coconut and lentil mixture. Simmer another 5 minutes.
☆ Remove from heat, sprinkle coriander and serve hot.

Note: If water reduces to less than 5 cups add more.

Cooking time: 1 hour 10 minutes   To serve: 4-6

Shorba-e-Anar

Pomegranate soup — A favourite soup of Moghul Emperors

4 cups (1 lt) pomegranate juice
12 spinach leaves, whole
1 tbsp white pepper powder

1 tsp ginger, grated
1 tsp chilli powder
1½ level tsps salt

1 tsp cumin seeds, roasted
and ground

☆ Heat the pomegranate juice and bring to a boil.
☆ Add rest of the ingredients together. Simmer over low heat for 7 minutes.
☆ Serve hot.

Cooking time: 15 minutes   To serve: 4-6   Picture on page: 22

Tuvar Dal Rasam

South Indian preparation — A thin highly spiced broth

1 cup (160 gms) tuvar dal (red gram)	½ tsp turmeric powder	**Ground to a paste**
2½ cups (575 ml) water	1 tsp oil	½ tsp whole black pepper
4 dry Kashmiri chillies	1 tsp coriander seeds	1 pinch of asafoetida
		1 pinch mustard seeds
		½ tsp cumin seeds
		2 tbsps coriander leaves, finely chopped
		2 level tsps salt
		1¼ cup (275 ml) tamarind pulp
		4 cups (1 lt) water

✩ Place water and dal together in a pan. Cook over medium heat unti soft. Add oil and turmeric powder.

✩ Dry roast, each separately, cumin seeds, black pepper (should start fuming), mustard seeds (must crackel) and dry red chillies. Grind them separately.

✩ Boil tamarind juice for 10 minutes until the raw smell disappears.

✩ Pour one litre water to the cooked dal with ground masala. Bring to a boil.

✩ Add asafoetida and coriander leaves, stir well. Serve hot in small individual glasses.

Cooking time: 30 minutes   To serve: 4-6

Mulligatawny Soup

Soup of pureed lentil, flavoured with spices and fresh herbs from South India

150 gm red gram dal, washed
1 fresh coconut, finely grated and milk extracted three times (see page 17)
3 medium onions, chopped
1 lime, squeeze out juice

1 × 1" piece ginger
2 cloves garlic
1 tbsp Madras curry powder (see page 20)
1 tbsp oil
1 sprig of curry leaves
A pinch of fenugreek powder

½ tsp black pepper
1½ tsps salt
4 tbsps boiled rice
2 tbsps coriander, finely chopped
1" piece cinnamon
2 lt (2000 ml) hot water

☆ Heat oil, saute onion, add dal, fry together.
☆ Add chopped garlic, ginger, curry leaves, fenugreek, cinnamon, curry powder, salt and pepper.
☆ Pour water, cover and cook till the dal is soft.
☆ Add coconut milk, strain the soup and add lime juice.
☆ Garnish with boiled rice and chopped coriander. Serve hot.

(Mutton stock can be substituted for water and diced fried mutton pieces for boiled rice.)

Cooking time: 40 minutes   To serve: 4-6   Picture on page: 67

Madras Kari Shorba

Lentil and vegetable soup of southern India

1 cup split peas or red lentil (masoor dal)
6 cups water
2 tbsps tamarind pulp (see page 20)
1 tbsp ground coriander
1 tbsp cumin seeds

½ tsp black pepper powder
½ tsp chilli powder
1½ tsps turmeric
Pinch of asafoetida (hing)
2½ cups chopped mixed vegetables (egg plant, beans, marrow and pumpkin)

2 green chillies, seeded and sliced
1 medium onion, finely sliced
2 level tbsps salt
½ tsp black mustard seeds
4 tbsps oil

* Wash and soak dal **overnight.**
* Drain and place in a sauce pan with water. Cook over medium heat until soft.
* Add tamarind pulp.
* Heat 2 tbsps oil in a pan. Fry the asafoetida and spices for a minute stirring constantly. Pour the dal mixture into this pan.
* Add vegetables. Heat remaining oil, fry mustard seeds, green chillies and onions until brown. Add to the soup with salt.
* Simmer 15 minutes more and serve.

Cooking time: 45 minutes   To serve: 4-6

Dahi ka Shorba

Yoghurt soup

2 cups (425 ml) vegetable stock or hot water
2 cups (500 ml) plain yoghurt, lightly beaten

2 tbsps lime juice
1½ level tsps salt
1 level roasted cumin seeds, ground
½ level tsp black pepper, ground

Dash of turmeric powder
⅝ cup (150 ml) cream (optional)
2 tbsps fresh mint leaves, finely chopped

* Heat the stock or water, bring to a boil. Reduce heat add yoghurt, stir constantly till well blended.
* Add all the seasoning except cream and mint. Simmer gently for 15 minutes.
* Add cream and chopped mint just before removing from heat. Serve hot.

Cooking time: 25 minutes   To serve: 4-6   Picture on page: 119

Phulka or Chapati

2 cups (225 gms) wheat flour (aata)	1 tsp salt	Ghee or butter
150 ml or ½ cup and 2 tbsps water	2 tbsps extra flour for rolling	

★ Sieve flour in a flat basin.

★ Add half the water, mix well and knead into a soft dough.

★ Knead for 15 minutes, gradually adding the remaining water and alternatively pressing and folding the dough. Now sprinkle 1 or 2 tbsps of water to it to swell for about half an hour.

★ Knead the dough again for 10 minutes, then divide the dough into 10 pieces and using a little dry wheat flour shape them into round balls.

★ Flatten each piece by placing it on the left palm and pressing it with the fingers of the right hand. Press it on a floured board, and roll out with a rolling pin into a thin pancake about 5″ (13 cms) diameter.

★ If you are using a chapati maker, then place the balls (one at a time) in the centre of the lower half then press with the upper half. And to prevent sticking sprinkle a little flour on the lower half of the chapati maker.

★ Heat the griddle and place the rolled chapati on it. Cook on medium heat for 30 seconds, and when one side dries up and tiny bubbles begin to appear, turn it over and cook till brown spots form on the under surface. Now remove the griddle from the fire, hold the chapati with a pair of tongs and place it directly over the heat till it swells up. In case of an electric cooking range turn the chapati over and as soon as brown spots appear on the under surface, press lightly around the edge with a folded soft cloth till it swells up completely.

★ Remove from the hot griddle, apply a little ghee or butter over one side. Serve immediately.

★ If chapaties are made in advance, they should be placed one above the other. Wrapped in a napkin and stored in a container.

Cooking time: 35 minutes	Makes: 10

Sada Paratha

2 cups (225 gms) wheat flour
3 tbsps ghee or butter

1 tsp salt
½ cup and 2 tbsps (150 ml) water

* Preparation of the dough is same as described under the chapati, then cover and keep aside for 10 minutes.
* Now divide the dough into 6 equal parts and shape them into round balls.
* Flatten and roll out into a flat disc about 5″ diameter.
* Now smear a little ghee, with a spoon on the roti (the upper surface only) and fold it over into a semi-circle. Smear some more ghee over the upper surface and fold it the second time. Double fold it lengthways press it gently with fingers and roll into a round circle making the edge thinner than centre.
* Place it on a hot griddle, turn over once and smear with ghee again.
* Cook for few seconds, turn over again and smear the other side with ghee as well.
* Cook for further few seconds until the paratha is golden brown on both sides. Serve hot.

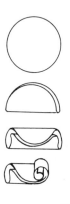

Cooking time: 20 minutes   Makes: 6

Makkai ki Roti (Maize Roti)

2 cups (225 gms) maize flour
(bhutte-ka-aata)
4 tbsps wheat flour

1 tsp salt
Warm water for kneading

2-3 tsps coriander leaves,
chopped
Ghee or oil for frying

* Sieve together maize flour, wheat flour and salt in a bowl, add coriander.
* Add enough warm water and knead well, make a smooth dough.
* Divide the dough into 8 equal parts, flatten it with your palm.
* Carefully roll out into a chapati size. Sprinkle extra flour to prevent sticking. Should be slightly thicker than paratha.
* Heat the griddle and place the roti, put 1 or 2 spoons of ghee or oil around it, then turn, cook the other side also in the similar manner.
* This roti should be served with butter, cream cheese or any vegetable dish. Serve hot, with sarson ka saag.

Cooking time: 25 minutes	Makes: 8	Picture on page: 67

Besan ki Roti

Northern India, Punjab and U.P.

4 cups (450 gms) gram flour (besan)
2 cups (450 ml) water

2 medium onions, chopped finely or grated
2 green chillies, chopped

3 tbsps coriander leaves,
chopped
Ghee or oil for shallow frying

* Sift flour in a bowl, add 2 tbsps ghee or oil, onions, chillies and coriander leaves. Mix well.
* Add warm water and knead well, make a stiff dough. Leave it for 20 minutes.
* Divide into 20 pieces and using a little dry flour (besan) shape them into round balls.
* Proceed as chapaties but make it a little thicker than chapaties (do not allow the onion to break up the roti).
* Heat the griddle, place the roti in the centre (cook one at a time) adding a little ghee to the edges. Remove when brown on both sides.

Cooking time: 40 minutes	Makes: 20	Picture on page: 67

Tandoori Roti

2 cups (225 gms) wheat flour   ½ tsp baking powder   50 gms ghee or butter
1 tsp salt   Warm water

* ☆ Sieve flour with salt and baking powder.
* ☆ Add half the ghee and mix well.
* ☆ Knead with your hand adding water very gradually. Keep the dough aside for 1½ hours. Covered with a wet towel.
* ☆ Knead the dough well again with your fist, divide into 8 balls. Now shape each ball. Pat and press the dough into a circle with your palm (not larger than size of a puri).
* ☆ Heat frying pan without any grease on it. Take bowl of clean water, wet your palm and rub water well on one side of the roti.
* ☆ Place (few rotis at a time) rotis in the fry pan, watered side down. Now turn it upside down over an open flame. Sprinkle water once or twice. Hold it for 3-4 minutes until lightly brown.
* ☆ This roti is traditionally made in a clay tandoor (baker's oven) in Punjab, but nowadays gas tandoors are available in any Indian food stores. If using gas tandoor, follow the above method.

Cooking time: 2 hours   Makes: 8   Picture on page: 34

Amritsar ka Paratha

2 cups (225 gms) wheat flour
1 level tsp salt
4 tbsps ghee

Water as required
Ghee for shallow frying
1 level tsp baking powder

For paste
3 tbsps plain flour
2 tbsps ghee

* Sift flour with salt and baking powder in a basin, mix ghee and add water slowly. Knead into a very soft dough. Cover with a damp cloth and leave aside for about 30 minutes.
* Beat together 3 tbsps plain flour and 2 tbsps ghee.
* Knead the dough well again, melt 1 tbsp ghee and gradually pour it in the dough, kneading all the time until the dough becomes very soft.
* Divide the dough into 8 equal parts.
* Roll out each part into a thin large circle like chapati and fold into half.
* Spread a thin layer of the paste on the folded chapati and fold it once again into half lengthwise. The chapati will now look like a thin long strip.
* Roll it up like a swiss roll, keeping the folds on the outerside, press and flatten to a round shape.
* Now roll each round lightly into a ¼" thick paratha.
* Heat ghee in a griddle. When the ghee is hot, shallow fry each paratha separately.

Cooking time: 45 minutes   Makes: 8

Mughlai Paratha

2 cups (225 gms) wheat flour
2 eggs beaten with ¼ tsp salt
and 1 tsp milk

1 tsp salt
2 tbsps ghee
1 tsp baking powder

Water for kneading
Ghee for shallow frying

* Sift flour, salt and baking powder together.
* Rub in 2 tbsps ghee and gradually add water. Make a stiff dough, knead well.
* Divide the dough in 6 equal parts and shape them into round balls.
* Roll out each round like a pancake about 6″ diameter. Coat the upper surface with a teaspoon of ghee and fold it over into a semicircle.
* Again spread little more ghee over the upper surface and double fold it lengthways. Press it lightly with the fingers.
* Roll it like a swiss roll keeping the folds on the outer side.
* Press it down, so as to form a flattened ball and roll out into a square (7″ × 7″).
* Brush the surface of each paratha with beaten eggs and turn all four corners towards the centre (centre should not be covered).
* Shallow fry one at a time on a hot griddle.

Cooking time: 25 minutes   Makes: 6

Khasta Roti

2 cups (225 gms) wheat flour
1-2 eggs, beaten
1 level tsp cumin seeds

1 level tsp salt
6 tbsps ghee or margarine
1 level tsp baking powder

5/8 cup (150 ml) milk

* Sieve flour and add the baking powder, salt, ghee and cumin seeds. Mix very well. Make into a dough using milk and eggs. Keep aside, covered for 20 minutes.
* Divide the dough into 6 equal parts and shape them into round balls.
* Now flatten and roll out each of the round into flat cake about 5″ (12 cms) diameter.
* Cook as parathas. Serve them hot.
* Khasta rotis should always be crisp.

Cooking time: 30 minutes   Makes: 6   Picture on page: 3

Shahi Roti

Northern India (U.P.)

2 cups (225 gms) plain white flour (maida)
1 level tsp salt
⅝ cup (150 ml) warm water
4 tbsps butter or ghee

2 tbsps extra flour
2 tbsps butter or ghee
Ghee or butter for shallow frying
3 tbsps almond paste

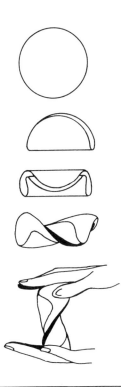

* Sieve flour and salt in a bowl.
* Add water and knead well. Make a soft dough. Cover with a damp cloth and keep aside for 30 minutes.
* Mix 4 tsps butter or ghee with 2 tsps flour, and almond paste. Beat well to make a paste.
* Knead the dough once again, melt 2 tsps butter or ghee and gradually pour it in the dough. Knead until the dough becomes very soft and pliable.
* Divide the dough into 6 equal parts. Roll each round into a thin large circle and fold it into half. Spread a thin layer of the paste on the folded circle and fold it once again into half, lengthways. The circle will now look like a thin long strip, shape into a spiral.
* Keeping the fold on the outer side, press and flatten to a ball and now make into a ¼" thick chapati with your palms.
* Heat the griddle, add a little butter or ghee and shallow fry each roti separately. Serve hot.

Cooking time: 20 minutes   Makes: 6

Bermi Roti

Jodhpuri

2½ cups (275 gms) wheat flour
2 cups (320 gms) split moong dal
(without skin), **soaked overnight**
225 gms spring onions with 5" stalks

2 level tsps salt
1 level tsp chilli powder
½ level tsp cumin seeds
Pinch of asafoetida

Water for kneading
Ghee

☆ Sift wheat flour with 1 tsp salt. Rub in ghee or oil with your finger tips until the mixture resembles coarse bread crumbs. Gently add water, gather the flour together to form a soft dough.

☆ Place the dough on a flat surface and knead to a smooth dough. Cover with a damp cloth and leave for half an hour.

☆ Clean, wash and finely slice the spring onions.

☆ Drain the dal and grind to a fine paste.

☆ Combine together the ground dal paste, onions, 1 tsp salt, chilli powder, cumin seeds and asafoetida. Mix thoroughly and keep aside.

☆ Knead the dough again. Divide into 9 parts — it will be little sticky so rub your hands with a little flour when handling it. Shape each part into a round ball,

☆ Roll each ball into a circle of 8" (20 cms) diameter, ¼" thickness. Dust your work surface with flour whenever necessary. Spread ¼ tsp ghee or oil over the surface of the roti.

☆ Place 2 heaped tbsps of dal mixture in the centre of the circle. Now carefully fold all four sides towards the centre leaving ½" space in between. Press it tightly to secure.

☆ Heat a griddle (tava) or a heavy fry pan. Place the roti (stuffed side facing down) dry fry for 2-3 minutes over low heat, turn over and cook the other side. Both the sides should have brown spots.

☆ Place the roti on a flat surface and pinch all the four sides of the stuffed side with your thumb and index finger, at ½" intervals. Each pinch should make a pair of dents. Return to fire, place the roti now on chapati holder (knitted wire round with a handle) and hold directly over the flame for few minutes until both the sides well cooked.

☆ Remove from heat and spoon ghee over the dents. Gently press the 4 corners towards centre so immediately all the ghee will be absorbed. Place again on the hot griddle, cook over low heat until both sides turn golden brown.

☆ Repeat with remaining dough.

Note: Bermi Roti is a complete meal in itself. Highly rich in protein, a popular bread of Jodhpur. The secret of making tasty Bermi Roti is the unique method of slow cooking.

Cooking time: 1 hour | Makes: 9 | Picture on page: 101

Baida Paratha

2 cups (225 gms) wheat flour	2 tbsps ghee or oil	Water to knead
2 tsps salt	½ tsp pepper	Ghee or oil for shallow frying
4 eggs, boiled and mashed	1 tsp coriander leaves, chopped	

* Sift wheat flour in a basin with 1 tsp salt. Gradually add water, make a stiff dough. Cover with a damp cloth. Keep aside for 20 minutes.
* Boil eggs and mash well. Add 1 tsp salt, pepper, coriander and 1 tsp ghee or oil. Mix thoroughly.
* Knead the dough until smooth. Divide into 8 equal parts and roll out each into 4″ diameter circle. Place 1 tbsp of egg filling in the centre of each circle. Shape them into round balls again.
* Now roll out each ball on a floured board to a circle of 5″ (13 cms) diameter. Rub little ghee or oil on one side.
* Heat a griddle, shallow fry each paratha with little ghee or oil. Cook until both the sides turn golden brown, turning once or twice.

Cooking time: 40 minutes   Makes: 6

Mughlai Roti

2 cups (225 gms) wheat flour	1 tsp aniseeds, powdered (saunf)	Ghee for frying
1 level tsp yeast (dry)	½ cup milk	Water for kneading
½ tsp salt	1 tsp sugar	

- Put warm milk in a bowl with sugar, then sprinkle yeast over it. Leave it for 20 minutes. Sieve flour with salt in a bowl, add aniseeds powder. Now pour the yeast mixture and knead well. Add little water if needed. Make a soft dough, cover it.
- Set aside in a warm place **for 2 hours.** Knead again and allow it to rise. Divide the dough into 10 equal parts, shape them into balls and roll out into rounds about 5″-6″ diameter (like phulkas).
- Now roast them until light brown, on a hot griddle.
- Before serving smear ghee on each hot roti.

Cooking time: 30 minutes   Makes: 10

Birahi Paratha

2 cups (225 gms) wheat flour
1 cup (100 gms) gram flour (besan)

1 tsp salt
½ tsp coriander powder

Water for kneading
Ghee or oil

☆ Sift wheat flour and salt in a bowl. Add water and make a stiff dough. Cover with damp cloth. Leave aside for 20 minutes.
☆ Mix besan and water separately and make a soft dough. Divide into 8 portions. Mould each portion into round balls.
☆ Knead again wheat flour dough. Divide into 8 equal parts. Roll out into the size of a puri and place one round besan ball in the centre of each puri. Cover bringing the edge over, shape them into round balls again.
☆ Now roll out each round to a circle of 5″ diameter.
☆ Heat the griddle on a low fire. Cook one at a time as plain parathas with very little ghee or oil. Fry until both the sides turn golden brown.

Cooking time: 40 minutes   Makes: 8

Ceylonese Roti

Madras

4 cups (450 gms) plain flour
1 tsp baking powder
1 tsp salt

150 gms fresh (or desiccated) coconut, grated
Warm water for kneading

Ghee or oil for shallow frying

☆ Sift flour with salt and baking powder in a bowl. Add coconut. Mix well. Slowly add water, knead to a soft dough and cover with a damp cloth. Keep aside for 30 minutes.
☆ Divide dough into 8 equal portions. Roll each into a ball. Roll out each ball into round disc 5″ (12 cms) diameter and ¼″ thickness, sprinkle with little flour if needed.
☆ Heat the griddle, lightly grease (use about 1 tsp ghee or oil), and cook one at a time, over low heat until brown specks appear on both sides. Remove from griddle, keep warm.
☆ Grease the griddle before each roti.
☆ Wrap in a piece of foil, keep until required. Reheat with the foil in oven.

Cooking time: 25 minutes   Makes: 8

Lachha Paratha

2 cups (225 gms) wheat flour
1 tsp salt

3 tbsps oil
Warm water for kneading

Oil for shallow frying

* Sieve flour and salt together in a bowl. Rub in 3 tbsps oil.
* Add water gradually, knead until smooth. Cover and leave aside for 20 minutes.
* Knead again and divide the dough into 2 portions. Shape each into a round ball. Flatten them a little.
* Roll out each flattened ball into a circle of 6″ (15 cms) diameter. Now cut it into 2″ strips lengthways. Place all the strips over the centre one.
* Roll like a swiss roll. Press a little with your fingers. Pour 1 tsp of oil on each.
* Take one at a time, roll it out into a round circle of 5″ diameter.
* As you remove, place it on your palms and lightly press towards the centre to show the layers clearly.
* Heat a griddle. Shallow fry one at a time like paratha. Serve hot with raita.

| Cooking time: 40 minutes | Makes: 8 | Picture on page: 154 |

Piaz ki Roti

Onion roti of Northern India (U.P.)

2 cups (225 gms) wheat flour
¼ level tsp soda bicarb
1 level tsp salt

3 medium onions, finely grated
6 green chillies, deseeded and chopped
2 tbsps mint leaves, finely chopped

Ghee or oil
Warm water for kneading

* Sift flour, soda and salt together in a bowl. Add all the chopped ingredients.
* Add water slowly mix well and knead to a smooth dough. Cover and keep aside for 20 minutes.
* Divide the dough into 6 portions. Shape them into round balls and roll out into 5″ (12 cms) diameter.
* Heat the griddle and shallow fry as parathas.
* Serve hot with raita and any vegetable dish.

| Cooking time: 30 minutes | Makes: 6 |

Khakhra

Gujarati crispy roti

1 cup (100 gms) wheat flour	1 level tsp garam masala	Ghee
1 cup (100 gms) plain white flour	4 tsps oil	Warm water or milk
1 level tsp salt		

* ☆ Sieve together wheat flour, white flour, salt and garam masala.
* ☆ Add oil and mix well, add enough warm water or milk and knead well make a soft dough and divide them into 8 equal parts.
* ☆ Roll the dough into very thin chapaties.
* ☆ Heat the griddle and cook the chapaties one at a time. Smear ghee on each and pile one on top of another.
* ☆ Take 2-3 chapaties and roast them on a hot griddle by pressing with a folded cloth on top. As each roti turns crisp on the under side, turn it and roast the other side till pinkish brown in colour. Similarly roast all the chapaties on a medium flame, applying pressure.
* ☆ This can be stored in an air tight box for some time.

Note: This roti is from Gujarat area. When people travel, this roti is carried by them for meals as 'Khakhras' remain fresh for many days. Eaten with pickle.

Cooking time: 30 minutes   Makes: 8

Gobi ka Paratha

A Bombay speciality

4 cups (450 gms) wheat flour
225 gms cauliflower
2 small onions, finely chopped
4 tbsps coriander leaves, finely chopped

1 green chilli, deseeded and chopped
½ inch ginger, chopped
2 tbsps lime juice
2 tbsps margarine or oil

Warm water for kneading
Ghee or oil for shallow frying
2 tsps salt

* Clean, wash and grate cauliflower. Place in a bowl. Pour hot water. Leave it for 5 minutes. Drain well. Squeeze the water out, add lime juice, chilli, 1 tsp salt, coriander, onions and ginger. Mix well, divide into 12 portions.
* Sift wheat flour with 1 tsp salt. Rub in margarine. Slowly add water and make a soft pliable dough. Cover with a damp cloth keep aside for 20 minutes.
* Knead the dough again, divide into 12 round balls. Roll out each into round disc 4" diameter. Place 1 portion of cauliflower mixture on each disc. Close up bringing the sides together carefully, shape into ball again.
* Place each ball on a floured board and roll out into a disc 5" (12 cms) diameter.
* Smear with ghee or oil one at a time. Shallow fry on a hot griddle until both the sides are golden brown in colour.

Cooking time: 40 minutes   Makes: 12

Phefre

Rajasthani farmers' bread

2 cups (225 gms) coarse wheat flour or jowar (barley flour)
1 tbsp cumin seeds, roasted and ground

2 level tsps salt
½ tsp baking powder
Water for kneading
75 gms ghee or melted butter

* Mix wheat flour with salt, cumin seeds, baking powder and enough water to make a stiff dough. Leave it aside for 20 minutes covered with a damp cloth.
* Knead well and make a smooth, pliable dough. Divide into 5 equal portions, shape them into round balls. Flatten lightly by pressing the centre with your thumb.
* Heat a griddle over medium heat. Place 2 flattened balls at a time without using fat, remove as they become hard.
* Place the flattened balls on a baking tray, bake in a pre-heated oven (375°F-190°C-Gas mark-5) for about 30 minutes, until cracks appear on top and colour turns light brown.
* Put ghee or melted butter in a small bowl. Very lightly press the centre of each phefre (flattened ball) and put it into the ghee or melted butter.
* Phefres are served hot with 'kari' or tuvar dal. Place one phefre in a plate, mash it with finger or fork, pour 1-2 tsps ghee or butter and little kari or dal over it.

Note: Phefre is one of the breads of Rajasthan. Traditionally made in 'Kandha' (dried cow dung fire) after cooking in a griddle. Easy to make and highly nutritious.

Cooking time: 60 minutes   Makes: 5   Picture on page: 120

Malwi Roti or 'Dopatri'

Madhya Pradesh

Ingredients A
3 cups (350 gms) plain flour
3 tbsps salad or veg. oil
1 tsp salt
¼ cup warm water

Ingredients B
100 gms bean sprouts
½ tsp salt
2 tomatoes, chopped
2 tsps oil
5 tsps water
½ tsp turmeric powder

* Sift flour with salt in a basin. Mix well with 2 tsps oil. Slowly add water, knead to a smooth dough.
* Divide the dough into 18 balls. Roll them out into 5″ (12 cms) diameter. Rub oil in one side of the round and place an ungreased round over it. Make sandwiches the same way.
* Heat a fry pan (ungreased) over low heat and cook the sandwiches both sides until pale brown specks appear. When cooked pull both halves apart.
* Put all the rotis in a steamer and steam for 10 minutes. Place them on a dry cloth.
* Heat rest of the oil in a pan. Saute bean sprouts. Add all B ingredients together. Cook for 5 minutes and remove from fire.
* Place the rotis in a plate and serve the bean sprouts in a bowl. Serve nariyal ki chutney as an accompaniment.

Cooking time: 20 minutes   Makes: 18

Dhakai Paratha

Shallow fried flaky bread of Bengal

2 cups (225 gms) plain flour
½ tsp salt
3 tbsps ghee or butter
2 tbsps extra flour

1 cup (100 gms) ghee or oil for frying
Water for kneading
Ghee or oil

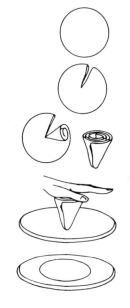

* ☆ Sieve flour and salt in a bowl.
* ☆ Mix well with 1 tbsp ghee or butter and make a soft pliable dough with water. Knead well.
* ☆ Divide dough into 6 portions. Roll out each portion into a round 5″ (12 cms) diameter like chapati.
* ☆ Smear with a little ghee and sprinkle with flour.
* ☆ Cut from the centre of the round to the edge. Roll from one edge to the other, forming a cone.
* ☆ Press the cone to form a flat round. Roll out into a 6″ (15 cms) round again. Repeat 3 times same way.
* ☆ Heat the griddle, fry the paratha with enough ghee until both the sides are brown and puff up.
* ☆ Serve these crisp parathas hot with any vegetable dish.

Cooking time: 20 minutes   Makes: 6

Bathuway ki Roti

Bihar

cups (225 gms) wheat flour	1 tsp salt	Warm water for kneading
50 gms bathuway or spinach	Oil or ghee	

- Clean, wash and boil bathuway or spinach with little water until tender. Drain well and grind to a paste.
- Sift salt and wheat flour in a bowl. Add bathuway or spinach paste and knead well.
- Add very little water if necessary, knead and make a smooth dough. Divide into 10 equal round balls.
- Roll them into round discs of 4"-5" diameter or make a triangle.
- Heat a griddle. Cook over low heat, applying 1 or 2 tsps oil or ghee around the roti while cooking. Cook until both the sides turn light brown.

Cooking time: 30 minutes	Makes: 10	Picture on page: 101

Chawal ki Roti

Rice flour roti of central India

½ cups (175 gms) fine rice flour	1" piece ginger	Oil or ghee for shallow frying
flakes garlic	3 tbsps plain yoghurt	
green chilli	1 tsp salt	

Grind, ginger, chilli and garlic to a smooth paste.
Mix well, salt, ginger paste and 2 tbsps oil or ghee with rice flour. Add yoghurt and make a stiff dough. Do not knead. Mix gently with fingers till a dough is formed.
Divide into 6 portions. Roll them out to a round disc of 3" (7½ cms) diameter and ¼" thickness.
Heat a griddle, shallow fry the rotis carefully one at a time, over a low heat. Cook until both the sides turn light brown in colour.

Cooking time: 20 minutes	Makes: 6

Methi ni Bhakhri

Traditional Gujarati roti

2 cups (225 gms) bajra flour *or* wheat flour
6 tbsps fenugreek leaves, cleaned and chopped

4 tbsps ghee
2 tsps green chillies, chopped finely
1 tsp sugar
½ tsp turmeric powder

1 tsp salt
Water for kneading
Ghee for frying

* Sift bajra or wheat flour and salt in a basin. Rub 2 tbsps ghee into the flour.
* Mix all the ingredients, knead to a soft dough with water.
* Divide the dough into 10 portions and roll out each into a circle of 3" (7½ cms) diameter.
* Place 2-3 bhakhris at a time on a hot griddle. Spoon little ghee around the bhakhris, turn and cook the other side, till both the sides are brown and crisp.
* It can be cooked without ghee also. In Gujarat, bhakhri roti is served for dinner with vegetable dish, milk and also with chutney during winter.

Cooking time: 15 minutes	Makes: 4-6

Kashmiri Roti

Taktaki

2¼ cups (250 gms) wheat flour
1 tsp salt
1 tsp pepper

½ tsp aniseeds (saunf)
½ tsp cumin seeds
A pinch of asafoetida

A pinch of carum (ajwain)
Warm milk for kneading
Oil or ghee for shallow frying

* Sift wheat flour with salt. Add pepper, aniseeds, cumin seeds, asafoetida and carum.
* Slowly pour enough warm milk, knead to a stiff dough. Sprinkle little water if the dough becomes too stiff.
* Divide the dough into 10-12 equal portions and roll out each portion into a disc of 3"-4" diameter and ¼" thick.
* Pierce the roti lightly with a fork. Cook on a hot griddle over low heat. Turn frequently, pu 1 or 2 tsps oil or ghee around the roti while cooking.
* Cook until both sides are turned brown.

Cooking time: 30 minutes	Makes: 10	Picture on page: 20

Sada Naan

Leavened bread of Northern India (U.P.)

cups (450 gms) plain flour	1 tbsp dried yeast	2 tbsps poppy seeds
⅔ cup (150 ml) milk or warm water	1 tsp sugar	1 tbsp sesame seeds
2 tbsps yoghurt	3 tbsp butter or ghee	2 tsps salt

* Sprinkle yeast and sugar into the hot milk or water, leave it for 20 minutes.
* Sift together flour, salt in a large bowl, and make a well in the centre. Put yoghurt and 2 tbsps butter with the yeast mixture. Knead well and leave it aside for 3-4 hours, in a warm place until it doubles in size.
* Punch down the dough and divide into 8 balls. Leave it to rest for 10 minutes.
* Roll out each ball in the shape of triangles or make a round disc. Then pull out one side to make like a teardrop shape.
* Mix together 1 tbsp ghee or butter, poppy seeds and sesame seeds.
* Spread a little of above mixture on each naan. Place them on a baking tray. Cook in a pre-heated oven (190°C-375°F-Gas Mark 5) for 4-5 minutes until brown specks appear.
* If the naan is not brown enough then put under a pre-heated grill for a minute or two.

Variation:

Badami Naan

2 cups almonds, blanched finely and shredded. Brush each sada naan with oil or butter before baking them. Sprinkle almonds and white sesame seeds on the greased side of every naan. Cook in a pre-heated oven for 4-5 minutes.

Cooking time: 40 minutes	Makes: 8	Picure on page: 154

Roghni Naan

4 cups (450 gms) plain white flour
1 tsp salt
1 cup (150 ml) warm milk
2 tbsps yoghurt
1 tbsp dry yeast or 25 gms fresh yeast

1 tsp sugar
4 tbsps butter or ghee
2 tbsps poppy seeds
1 tbsp sesame seeds
1 egg, beaten (optional)

For glazing
10 strands of saffron
2 tbsps milk

* ☆ Mix 2 tbsps milk and saffron strands in a cup. Leave it aside.
* ☆ Sift flour and salt in a bowl and make a well in the centre. Mix warm milk and butter or ghee together and pour it in the centre. Sprinkle yeast and sugar over it. Let it stand for 30 minutes.
* ☆ Knead for 15-20 minutes. Add beaten egg (if using) and yoghurt. Knead again until dough is smooth and elastic. Form the dough into a ball and let it rest for 15 minutes.
* ☆ Grease a clean bowl. Place the dough in it. Cover with a dry cloth. Allow it to rise **for 6 hours.** For best result leave it **overnight.**
* ☆ Next morning punch down the dough and knead again. Divide the dough into 8 portions. Shape them into round ball. Leave it to rest for 15 minutes.
* ☆ Pre-heat the oven to very hot (450°F-230°C-Gas Mark 8).
* ☆ Take one ball of dough at a time and roll out the dough into a round circle. Keep them thin in the centre and thicker around the edges. Then pull one end outward, making a tear-drop shape.
* ☆ Brush with ghee and saffron solution and sprinkle poppy seeds or sesame seeds.
* ☆ Brush the baking trays with water. Now place 2-3 naans on each baking tray. Bake for 4-5 minutes until they puff up and brown specks appear on top.

| Cooking time: 40 minutes | Makes: 8 | Picture on page: 68 |

Shahjehani Naan

1 recipe of sada naan (page 63)	1 tomato, deseeded, chopped	8 tbsps tomato sauce
175 gms kheema, boiled	1 tsp salt	1 tbsp parsley or coriander
1 onion, finely chopped	½ tsp pepper	leaves, chopped
4 flakes of garlic, chopped	1 tsp poppy seeds	2 tbsps oil

* Heat oil, fry onion and half the garlic till lightly browned. Add tomato and kheema. Stir well, add salt and pepper. Cook for 5-6 minutes. Sprinkle half parsley or coriander and remove from heat.
* Prepare the dough for naan as directed in the recipe of sada naan. Divide the dough into 8 equal portions. Shape each part into round ball, flatten a little and make a depression in the centre. Place 1 tbsp of stuffing and shape into a ball.
* Roll them out to an oblong. Shape into teardrop by pulling one side after rolling it out to a thick oblong or make a plain triangle.
* Brush with tomato sauce, sprinkle poppy seeds, garlic and coriander.
* Bake in a pre-heated oven (230°C-450°F-Gas Mark 5) for 4-5 minutes until brown specks appear or put under hot grill.

Cooking time: 25 minutes   Makes: 8

Pudina ka Roti

Mint roti

2 cups (225 gms) wheat flour	2 tbsps ghee	Water for kneading
tsp salt	1 cup mint, ground to a paste	Ghee for frying

* Sift flour and salt in a bowl, rub ghee evenly, add water and make a stiff dough.
* Add mint paste and mix well. Knead again. Keep aside for 30 minutes.
* Divide the dough into 10 parts. Shape them with your palm and flatten it.
* Roll each part into a round, like chapati.
* Place one at a time, on a hot griddle and shallow fry with ghee, like paratha.

Cooking time: 35 minutes   Makes: 10

Khameera Naan

4 cups (450 gms) flour
1 egg, beaten (optional)
150 ml or ½ cup and 2 tbsps milk

3 tsps khameer (see page 17)
1 tsp salt
1 tsp poppy seeds

1 tsp aniseeds
Ghee
1 tbsp butter

* **Make khameer 1 night before.**
* Sieve flour and salt, add aniseeds and butter. Mix well with fingers.
* Gradually add egg, warm milk, khameer and knead thoroughly. Cover and leave the dough in a warm place **for 2 hours.**
* Divide the dough into 10 equal parts and shape them into balls with the help of dry flour. Cover and leave them for 15 minutes.
* Flatten each ball into a pancake by tossing it from one hand to the other. Now pull one side gradually to make a triangle or oval shape.
* Brush with ghee and sprinkle poppy seeds on one side and a little warm water on the other. Stick the moistured surface of the pancake to the hot wall of the clay oven (tandoor).
* You can use an electric or gas tandoor (which is available in market) or you can use a griddle after applying warm water and ghee.
* Place the pancake on a hot griddle, the moistured side down. When the lower surface is baked, invert the griddle along with naan over direct heat and allow the upper surface to cook. Serve this roti with any barbecued dish.

Cooking time: 45 minutes   Makes: 10

Facing Page
Clockwise:

Vegetarian Kulcha
Rubian Tandoori
Makkai ki Roti
Besan ki Roti
Mulligatawney
Dhingri Chole
Sarson-da-Saag
Murgh Badami
Boondi ka Raita
Sada Puri

Taftan

Leavened bread with milk, yoghurt and eggs from U.P.

4 cups (450 gms) plain flour
25 gms fresh yeast *or*
4 tsps dry yeast
2 tbsps plain yoghurt

3 tsps sugar
2 tsps salt
2 eggs, beaten (optional)

2 tbsps poppy seeds *or*
black onion seeds (kalonji)
150 ml or ½ cup and 2 tbsps
milk
25 gms oil or ghee

☆ Sprinkle yeast and sugar over warm milk. Leave in a warm place until it starts to froth.
☆ Sift flour in a bowl, with salt. Make a well in the centre. Pour the yeast mixture with yoghurt, beaten eggs and 2 tbsps oil. Mix well.
☆ Knead well for 15 minutes until the dough is smooth and elastic. Rub oil in a warm large bowl. Place the dough, cover and leave it to prove **for 6-8 hours.**
☆ Knead the dough again. Divide into 8 equal portions and shape them into balls. Keep aside again for 20 minutes.
☆ Pat the dough into a circle with your palm, keeping them thin in the centre and thicker around the rim. Now pull one side of the naan to give it the shape of a tear drop. If you cannot make the tear drop shape, then shape the naans into triangulars.
☆ Brush the top with melted ghee or oil and sprinkle poppy seeds or black onion seeds. Place them in the baking tray.
☆ Bake in a pre-heated oven (190°C-375°F-Gas Mark 5) for 2-4 minutes until brown specks appear.

Note: Taftan naan can be made perfectly also under hot grills. If you are using a tandoor then wet one side and stick wet side to the tandoor and close it.

Cooking time: 25 minutes   Makes: 8

Facing Page
Clockwise:

Roghni Naan
Kheema Naan
Khubani ki Chutney
Gosht Akbari
Hassan
Kathi Roll of Calcutta (centre)

Rotlee

Roti Gujarati style

2 cups (225 gms) wheat flour 1 tsp salt	3 tbsps ghee or oil Warm water for kneading	Ghee

* Sift flour twice. Add salt, rub in fat. Mix well for 10 minutes.
* Gradually add water, mix thoroughly. Knead to a soft dough.
* Divide dough into 15 equal balls and roll out each one into a round disc 7" (18 cms) diameter.
* Cook them in a hot griddle, turning the roti once, without any fat for 1 minute. Then holding with a tong place directly over open flame for few seconds. It puffs up immediately. Turn once. Remove from heat.
* Apply ghee evenly on one side. Keep in a closed container. Repeat the same with rest.
* Rotlees are thinner and softer than phulkas or chapaties. While keeping it should be placed on top of another.

Cooking time: 25 minutes   Makes: 15

Chilla Puri

A recipe from Sind

1 cup (100 gms) wheat flour or plain flour 1 onion, grated	1 green chilli, finely chopped 1 tbsp coriander leaves, finely chopped	1 level tsp salt ½ cup and 2 tbsps (150 ml) cold water Ghee or oil

* Sift flour and salt together in a bowl. Gradually pour all water and mix well. Beat until smooth. Leave it aside for 20 minutes.
* Beat again and add onion, chilli and coriander leaves. Mix well.
* Heat a griddle. Put a tsp of ghee or oil. Pour 2 tbsps of batter and spread it evenly. Make a round circle 4" (10 cms) diameter. Turn once. Cook other side. Add 1 or 2 tsps of ghee or oil if necessary. Cook until both sides turns light brown.
* Repeat the same with remaining batter. Serve hot with mint chutney or pickle.

Cooking time: 30 minutes   Makes: 6

Sheer-Mal

From northern India

4 cups (450 gms) plain flour
4 tsps dry yeast
1 tsp salt
40 gms castor sugar
2 eggs, beaten (optional)
1 cup (250 ml) warm milk

2 cups (220 gms) khoa (dried whole milk), mashed
25 gms seedless raisins
100 gms double cream
2 tbsps poppy seeds
225 gms ghee or butter

½ tsp kewra essence (or rose)
Extra milk
1 tsp saffron, soaked in 1 tbsp warm milk

* Heat milk, do not boil, sprinkle yeast and sugar over it.
* Sieve flour, salt in a large bowl. Add eggs, raisins, khoa, double cream and half the ghee with yeast mixture.
* Mix well and knead to a smooth dough. Add essence, if the dough is stiff then sprinkle little extra milk and knead again. Cover with a damp cloth. Keep in a warm place to rise **for 8 hours.** For best results leave it **overnight.**
* Punch down the dough and knead again. Divide into 8 equal parts. Shape them into round balls.
* Place each round in a floured board, roll out into round thick circle. Leave aside for 20 minutes until it becomes double its size. Each circle should not be bigger than size of a dinner plate.
* Prick all over the roti with a fork, leaving 1" margin around. Brush melted ghee or butter and saffron solution. Sprinkle poppy seeds.

Bake in a pre-heated moderate oven (180°C-350°F-Gas Mark 4) until the roti turns light brown in colour.

Sprinkle little cold milk over them when they are half done, put them back to the oven for a few minutes more.

Remove from oven and sprinkle cold milk well over both sides, as this makes the roti soft.

Wrap with foil or butter paper. Keep until required. Reheating can be done with the foil. This roti can be kept for 4-5 days.

Cooking time: 45 minutes | Makes: 8 | Picture on page: 171

Roomali Roti

1½ cups (175 gms) wheat flour
50 gms plain flour

1 tsp salt
Cold water for kneading

2 tbsps melted ghee or oil

* Sift wheat flour, plain flour and salt together in a bowl. Rub in ghee or oil. Slowly add water and make a soft dough. Keep it covered with a damp cloth for 30 minutes. Dough should be very smooth and elastic.
* Knead well again. Divide the dough into 6 portions. Shape them into round balls.
* Roll out each ball on a floured board to a round disc. Now place the disc on back of your palms (palms facing down). Circle your wrist slowly anti-clockwise motion. Try to swing the roti in the air, again let it land on back of your palms. Make a large very thin circle 12″ (30 cms) diameter.
* Expert chefs swing the roti in the air and make roomali rotis as large as a bicycle wheel. needs a lot of practice to make this roti.
* It should be as thin as tissue and expanded well.
* Heat griddle inverted (upside down). Place the rotis carefully over the inverted griddle, spread evenly. This roti takes hardly 1 minute to cook. It should be folded like a handkerchief.

Cooking time: 45 minutes   Makes: 6

Baqarkhani Naan

4 cups (450 gms) plain flour
/2 cup (100 gms) double cream
4 tsps dry yeast
4 tsp salt
4 tsp cardamom powder
4 tbsp sugar

2 eggs (optional)
3¾ cups (885 ml) warm milk
1 cup (180 gms) ghee or butter
1 cup (110 gms) khoa (dried whole milk)

2 tbsps poppy seeds
½ tsp kewra essence or 1 tsp rose water
Extra ghee or butter for frying

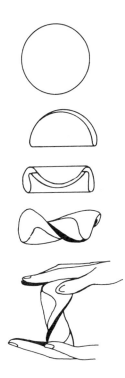

* Heat 1 cup milk, do not boil and sprinkle yeast and sugar over it. Leave it to froth for 20 minutes.
* Sift flour, salt in a large bowl. Rub in 180 gms ghee or butter. Add khoa, eggs, cream and cardamom. Mix well. Gently add yeast mixture and remaining milk. Knead well to a smooth dough.
* Take a clean bowl. Rub oil. Place the dough and cover with a damp cloth. Leave **overnight** for best results or **8 hours** in a warm place until it is double of its original size.
* Punch down the dough, add rose water and knead again. Divide into 10 equal parts.
* Roll out each of them on a floured board to a large circle then spread 2 tsps of melted ghee or butter lightly, fold it into half, again spread a layer of ghee or butter on the folded circle. Fold it once again into half, lengthways. It will now look like a long strip. Now twist the strip into a spiral. Keeping the fold on the outer side. Press and flatten to a ball. Now roll out to large discs (the size of a dinner plate), of the same thickness as the naan.
* Heat 1 or 2 tbsps ghee or butter in a griddle, cook one at a time and drizzle more ghee or butter on top of them as they cook. Sprinkle poppy seeds.
* Serve hot with vegetable dish.

Note: The traditional method of making Baquarkhani is little different and known as 'Dum Cooking'. In this method the tava is placed over a medium charcoal fire, and naan is covered. Layers of burning coals are placed on top of the lid. The result is a combination of frying and pressure cooking. Barquarkhani is a richer version of 'Sheer-Mal'.

Cooking time: 45 minutes   Makes: 10

Bombay Roti or Andey ki Roti

2 cups (225 gms) wheat flour
100 gms minced meat or vegetarian
kheema (see page 18)
2 tsps salt

4 green chillies, deseeded and
chopped
4 tbsps coriander leaves, chopped
4 tbsps mint leaves, chopped
8 eggs

Water for kneading
Ghee or oil for shallow frying

* Boil minced meat or vegetable kheema with 1 tsp salt until tender. Remove from heat. Divide into 8 portions.
* Sift wheat flour with 1 tsp salt. Add water slowly. Mix well and knead to a soft pliable dough. Keep aside for 20 minutes, covered with a damp cloth.
* Knead again the dough and divide into 8 equal portions. Shape them into balls.
* Lightly flour a board and pat out each ball into a square 5″ × 5″.
* Mix minced meat with coriander, mint, green chillies.
* Spread one portion of minced meat over the dough only in centre. Pat and pull out a little to make it thin (6″ × 6″) size.
* Beat lightly one egg and pour in the centre of the disc. Spread evenly over the mixture. Now fold the empty 4 sides over towards the centre. Cook over low heat. Shallow fry with ghee or oil until both the sides are light brown in colour.
* Spread egg after placing the roti on griddle, fry on a hot griddle.
* Repeat same with remaining dough.

| Cooking time: 30 minutes | Makes: 8 | Picture on page: 172 |

Dal Puri

2 cups (225 gms) wheat flour
50 gms moong dal
50 gms gram dal

2 cardamoms, shell removed
½ tsp cumin seeds
1 tsp salt

1 tsp garam masala
Water for kneading
Ghee or oil for deep frying

* Soak both dals **overnight,** drain and grind to a paste with cardamom and cumin seeds.
* Heat 2 tbsps oil fry the dal paste, add salt and garam masala.
* Sift wheat flour, add 1 tbsp ghee or oil and enough water. Knead well and make a soft dough.
* Divide into 16 round balls. Flatten a little, place 1 tsp of fried dal, shape into a round ball again.
* Roll out each ball into a circle of 3″ (7½ cms) diameter. (This puri is slightly thicker).
* Heat ghee or oil in a heavy pan. Deep fry puris one or two at a time. Turn once. Remove when colour turns golden brown.

Cooking time: 20 minutes   Makes: 16

Masala Roti

1 cup (100 gms) wheat flour
100 gms Bengal gram flour (besan)
1 tsp salt
2 medium tomatoes, seeds removed and chopped finely

1 green chilli, chopped
2 tbsps ghee
1 tsp black pepper
1 tbsp coriander, chopped
1 large onion, chopped

Warm water for kneading
Ghee for shallow frying

* Sift in a bowl, wheat flour and gram flour with salt.
* Add 2 tbsps ghee, rub well with fingers, add tomatoes, chilli, black pepper, onion and coriander.
* Gradually add warm water, knead into a stiff dough, leave aside for 30 minutes covered.
* Divide dough into 6 equal parts. Now roll out each portion slowly like chapati but make it little thicker than a chapati or the roti will break.
* Heat a griddle, keep a low flame and shallow fry one at a time. Turn very carefully. Serve hot with yoghurt or chutney.

Cooking time: 40 minutes   Makes: 6

Yehudi Roti

Jewish roti. A speciality of Bombay

4 cups (450 gms) plain flour
3 tbsps khameer *Or*
4 level tsps dry yeast

1 tsp sugar
1 tbsp salt
2 tbsps oil

1 cup (250 ml) warm water
Little extra oil for brushing

☆ Sprinkle sugar, yeast over warm water. Leave it to froth for 20 minutes.
☆ Sieve flour in a bowl. Make a well in the centre. Pour the yeast liquid and oil; mix well and knead to a soft dough. Cover the dough. Leave in a warm place to prove **for 2 hours** until double in size.
☆ Knead well again. Divide into 6 equal portions. Shape into round balls.
☆ Roll each ball into a round disc 10″ diameter. It should be rolled paper thin in the middle and slightly thicker towards the sides. Place them in a baking tray.
☆ Brush the top with oil and bake in a pre-heated hot oven (400°F-200°C-Gas Mark 6) for 5-7 minutes till the roti turns crisp.
☆ It can be cooked under hot grill also. To be served immediately.

Note: This roti is another delight of Bombay breads. Traditionally this roti is made in a tandoor. The flattened circular roti is placed on a larger round hard board and it is stretched out to cover the surface. Then the board is swung into the tandoor so that the roti sticks to the wall of the tandoor and the board is removed. When the roti is cooked, it is removed by a pair of tongs. It has a crisp centre for making it thinner in the middle.

This was made by the 'Jews' of Bombay, who had migrated from Baghdad, so the roti is called 'Yehudi roti' (Jewish roti).

Cooking time: 35 minutes   Makes: 6   Picture on page: 172

Muslim Naan

From Surat

4 cups (450 gms) plain flour
1 level tsp salt
1 tsp sugar

2 tsps dry yeast
2 tbsps yoghurt
3 tbsps oil or butter

1 cup (250 ml) warm milk or water

* Mix yeast with sugar and warm milk or water. Leave it for 20 minutes.
* Sift together flour and salt in a large bowl and make a well in the centre and put yoghurt, 2 tbsps oil or butter with the yeast mixture. Knead well and leave it aside for **3-4 hours** in a warm place until it doubles in size.
* Punch down the dough and knead well again.
* Divide the dough into 6 portions. Roll out into a round disc of 6" diameter. Leave it to prove again until double in size. Brush the top with remaining oil.
* Place them in a baking tray. Bake in a pre-heated oven (450°F-230°C-Gas Mark 5) for 5-6 minutes until the top turns brown in colour. Again brush oil lightly over the sloping dark brown tops.

Cooking time: 35 minutes	Makes: 6	Picture on page: 172

Lasan ki Roti

Garlic roti

cups (225 gms) wheat flour
pod garlic, finely chopped
level tsp salt

1 level tsp cumin seeds, roasted and ground
2 tbsps ghee, melted

Water for kneading
Ghee for frying

- Sift flour with salt in a basin.
- Rub in ghee, add cumin seeds and garlic.
- Slowly add water and knead to a soft dough. Keep aside for 20 minutes.
- Divide dough in 5 parts and proceed as with paratha.
- Serve hot with any dal.

Cooking time: 25 minutes	Makes: 5	Picture on page: 154

Sada Bhatura

Deep fried bread of Punjab

1 cup whole wheat flour	1 level tsp soda bicarb	½ tsp salt
1 cup plain flour	1 tsp sugar	Ghee or oil for deep frying
3 tbsps sour curds	1 egg (optional)	
1 tbsp ghee	8 tbsps warm water	

Note: All ingredients should be warm.

☆ Sieve together flour, wheat flour, soda, salt in a bowl.

☆ Add ghee, egg, sugar, warm curds and warm water to make it into a soft dough.

☆ Continue kneading the dough till it does not stick to the fingers or on the side of the bowl

☆ Cover with a damp cloth and leave it to swell in a warm place or over a pan of hot water **for 5-6 hours.**

☆ Divide it into 10 equal parts, shape into balls and roll out into rounds about 4″ (10 cms) diameter. Keep them covered in a large tray.

☆ Fry them one at a time in smoking hot ghee or oil, till it puffs up and turns light brown.

Cooking time: 25 minutes   Makes: 10

Masala Bhatura

1 recipe of plain bhatura
2 tbsps green chillies, seeds
removed and chopped

2 tbsps onion, finely chopped
2 tbsps parsley or coriander leaves,
chopped

1 tsp garam masala or all spice

* Prepare dough as per method given for sada bhatura.
* Add chillies, onion, parsley and garam masala just before adding water.
* Rest make same as plain bhatura.
* Serve hot with chole, potato curry or chutney.

Variations:

Vegetarian kheema bhatura: Mix one recipe of plain bhatura and 1 cup boiled kheema or minced nuggets. Add 2 tbsps finely chopped onion, green chillies as desired, coriander leaves and salt. Make rest as plain bhatura.

Meetha bhatura: Add 3 tbsps sugar and 1 tsp cardamom powder to the plain bhatura dough. Proceed as plain bhatura.

Cooking time: 25 minutes   Makes: 10

Bhature

Plain flour leavened, deep fried bread Ludhiana style

4 cups (450 gms) white flour	6 tbsps warm water	1 level tsp baking powder
1 cup (250 ml) yoghurt, warmed *Or*	1 level tsp salt	1 tbsp ghee
4 tbsps yoghurt & 1 egg	1 level tsp sugar	Oil for deep frying

* ★ Sieve together flour, baking powder and salt into a large bowl.
* ★ Add egg (if using), sugar, yoghurt and enough warm water to make a soft dough till it does not stick to the fingers or to the side of the bowl.
* ★ Apply 1 tbsp ghee to the hand and continue kneading till the dough becomes pliable. Cover it with a damp cloth and leave it to swell in a warm place **for 2 hours.**
* ★ Divide the dough into 12 equal parts, shape into round balls and roll out each ball into a round about 4″ (10 cms) diameter. Keep them covered in a tray.
* ★ Heat the oil and fry bhature one or two at a time until it puffs up. Turn and cook other side for few seconds. Drain and keep on a kitchen paper.

Cooking time: 30 minutes	Makes: 12	Picture on page: 34

Batia Roti

Rajasthani salted roti

2 cups (225 gms) wheat flour
2 tbsps ghee
2 tbsps coriander, chopped

1 tbsp cumin seeds, roasted and ground
1 tbsp salt

1 tbsp black pepper
Water for kneading

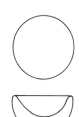

* Sift flour in a basin and make a soft dough with water, leave the dough covered with a damp cloth for 30 minutes.
* Knead again and divide the dough into 8 parts.
* Roll out each part into a disc about 5″ (12 cms) diameter.

* Spread evenly (a little of each) cumin seeds, salt, pepper, coriander and ghee. Now roll it like a swiss roll, twist it into a spiral. Keeping the folds on the outer side, press and flatten to a ball.
* Roll out lightly into ¼″ thick round disc 5″ (12 cms) diameter.
* Cook on a hot griddle with very little ghee or oil, also can be cooked without fat. Serve hot with any vegetable or pulse dish.

Cooking time: 40 minutes   Makes: 8

Dosai

South Indian bread

2 cups (225 gms) ground rice
1 tbsp wheat flour or semolina (suji)
1 tsp salt

75 gms husked split black beans (urad dal)
A pinch of soda bicarb
Water for blending
Ghee for frying

For filling
4 potatoes, boiled, peeled and mashed
3 medium onions, chopped finely
1 green chilli (optional)
¼ tsp turmeric powder
½ tsp mustard seeds
1 tsp salt
1 sprig of curry leaves
2 tsps oil

☆ Soak rice and dal separately in cold water **overnight.**
☆ Next day drain and grind rice in electric blender, adding very little water to facilitate blending.
☆ Strain through a sieve and discard the rough residue.
☆ Grind the dal same way but do not strain.
☆ Mix both the paste in a bowl, add salt, semolina and soda, cover and keep it in a warm place for **6 hours.** Stir well time to time.
☆ Heat oil, fry mustard seeds, onion, green chilli. Add turmeric powder and curry leaves.
☆ Add potatoes and salt, mix well and sprinkle little water, remove trom fire.
☆ Beat the dosai mixture well, if it is too thick, then add little water and beat again. The mixture should be pouring consistency.
☆ Heat the dosai griddle or plain griddle. Heat should be moderate. Smear lightly with ghee or oil and pour in about ⅓ cup of batter. It should cover the bottom of the griddle thinly. Spread the batter with the back of a wooden spoon or an Indian katori.
☆ Cover and cook for 1-2 minutes. Remove cover, cook for another 1-2 minutes. Place 2 tbsps of potato mixture in the centre of the dosai and fold like an omelette. Put a little ghee or oil, on the sides of the griddle and turn the dosa over and fry another ½ minute. Serve hot with sambar and nariyal chutney.

Cooking time: 50 minutes	Makes: About 18	Picture on page: 119

Banjara Roti

Gypsy roti

2 cups (225 gms) Bajri flour
or millet flour
1 tsp salt

2 green chillies, chopped
1 tsp ginger, chopped
½ cup yoghurt

6 cloves garlic, crushed
Cold water for kneading
Ghee or oil

* Sieve flour and salt.
* Mix well with yoghurt, garlic, green chillies, ginger.
* If needed add little water and make a stiff dough.
* Divide the dough into 6 portions. Roll out into ½" thick circles.
* Heat a griddle, place the roti in the centre. Cook 2-3 minutes then turn the roti. Take a spoon of ghee and put around the roti.
* Cook until both sides turn light brown. Serve hot with any vegetable dish.

Cooking time: 25 minutes	Makes: 6	Picture on page: 223

Puri Patiala

Patiala style of Punjab

cups (225 gms) plain flour
level tbsps semolina (suji)
tbsps rice flour

1 tsp salt
½ tsp turmeric powder
3 tbsps ghee or oil

Ghee for deep frying
Water for kneading

- Sieve together, flour, semolina, turmeric powder and salt. Rub 3 tbsps ghee to the flour mixture. Add water slowly and knead to a soft dough.
- Beat 1 tbsp ghee and rice flour together until creamy.
- Knead the dough again, and roll out into a thick round. Spread rice flour paste.
- Cut puris about 2" diameter with a biscuit cutter.
- Heat ghee in a pan over a low flame.
- Deep fry puris 1 or 2 at a time, until golden colour. Serve hot with any vegetable dish.

Cooking time: 20 minutes	Makes: 18

Puran Poli

Lentil-stuffed sweet roti of Maharashtra

2 cups (225 gms) wheat flour	50 gms sugar	Ghee or butter for frying
1 cup (160 gms) red gram (tuvar dal)	1 tsp cardamom powder	Water for kneading
2 tbsps oil	3 cloves	

★ Sieve flour, add oil and enough water gradually and knead to a smooth dough. Make 6 equal size balls and keep aside covered with a muslin.

★ Boil the dal in a pan with 1½ cups of water. Cook till tender. Drain off the water and add sugar, cardamom and cloves. Stir well until sugar melts and the mixture is completely dry.

★ Grind the mixture to a paste, roll into balls of the same number and about the same size of the flour balls.

★ Flatten out and slightly roll the flour balls. Place a ball of the dal mixture in the centre and cover completely with the flour dough. Shape into a smooth, large circle.

★ Place on a floured rolling board and roll out into a round pancake about ⅛" thick and 6" (15 cms) diameter.

★ Heat the griddle. Place one roti at a time cook for a minute, turn it, take a spoon of ghee and put it around the roti. Turn again, cook until both the sides are crisp and golden brown.

★ Cook all the rotis same way. Serve hot with any vegetable curry.

Cooking time: 20 minutes   Makes: 6

Vegetarian Kheema Kulcha

2 cups (225 gms) plain flour
2 level tsps dry yeast
1 tsp sugar
1 tsp salt
4 tbsps plain yoghurt
2 tbsps oil

4 tbsps warm milk
2 tsps poppy seeds
1 extra egg or milk
Water for kneading
Ghee for shallow frying

For filling
1 cup (225 gms) vegetarian minced meat, cooked (see page 18)
50 gms cheese, grated
2 flakes garlic, chopped
2 tbsps oil
1 tsp salt

- Sprinkle yeast and sugar over warm milk and leave it in a warm place for 20 minutes.
- Sift flour and salt in a bowl. Make a well in the centre, pour beaten egg, yeast mixture, yoghurt and oil. Mix well and knead to a soft dough. Cover with a damp cloth and keep in a warm place **for 6 hours** until the dough is double in size.
- Heat oil in a pan, add garlic, fry for 2 minutes. Add minced meat and cheese with salt. Saute for 5 minutes and remove from heat.
- Punch down the dough again, knead well. Divide into 8 equal portions. Shape them into round balls.
- Make a depression in the centre of each round. Place 1-2 tbsps of filling and shape them into round balls again.
- Roll out each ball into thick round disc 4" (10 cms) diameter. Place them in a baking tray and leave it to rise again for 30 minutes. Brush lightly with beaten egg.
- Bake in a pre-heated oven (220°C-425°F-Gas Mark 7) for 8 minutes. Remove and shallow fry like paratha for 1 minute.

Cooking time: 20 minutes   Makes: 8   Picture on page: 67

Phulko Luchi

Puffy deep fried bread of Bengal

2 cups (225 gms) plain flour   1 tsp salt   Ghee for deep frying
2 tbsps ghee or oil   Warm water for kneading

* Sieve flour with salt in a bowl.
* Add ghee and mix well with your finger tips. Slowly add water little at a time. Knead to a stiff dough.
* Divide the dough into 20 equal portions and shape them into round balls.
* Grease lightly the flour board and rolling pin. Now roll out each round into a thin pancake about 3″ (7.5 cms) diameter.
* Heat ghee in a pan to smoking point. Then drop the rolled pancakes, one at a time gently into it.
* Turn over immediately and press with a perforated wire frying slice (poni) till it swells up and acquires a light brown colour.
* Remove from ghee and drain on a kitchen paper. Serve hot with aloo ki sabzi.

Cooking time: 20 minutes   Makes: 20

Amritsar ki Luchi

Deep fried crispy bread

4 cups (450 gms) plain flour   1 level tsp baking powder   2 tbsps ghee or oil
1 level tsp salt   Water for kneading   Ghee or oil for deep frying

* Sieve flour, salt and baking powder together in a bowl. Add 2 tbsps ghee or oil, mix well.
* Slowly add water and make a pliable dough, divide into 10 portions, shape with your palm into round balls.
* Now roll out each round ball into a large circle 9″ (23 cms) diameter.
* Heat ghee or oil in a large pan or karhai and deep fry one at a time. Turn once until both the sides are golden colour and crisp.
* Serve hot with chutney and aloo ki sabzi.

Cooking time: 10 minutes   Makes: 10

Radhabalobhi Luchi

Deep fried bread of West Bengal

2 cups (225 gms) plain flour
25 gms urad dal flour
2 tbsps ghee or oil

1 tsp salt
1 tsp aniseeds, ground
Water for kneading

Ghee for deep frying

* Sieve the flour with salt.
* Add dal flour, aniseeds and 2 tbsps ghee. Mix well with your finger tips.
* Add slowly water and knead well. Make a smooth dough, leave it aside for 20 minutes.
* Divide the dough into 8 equal parts and shape them into round balls. Flatten and roll out each into a flat pancake about 5″ (13 cms) diameter. Smear the upper surface with little ghee.
* Heat ghee in a pan. Fry each rolled out luchi, one at a time. Serve hot with any vegetable dish and pickle.

Cooking time: 30 minutes   Makes: 8

Shehad ki Roti

Honey roti

2 cups (225 gms) plain flour or wheat flour
1/2 cup and 2 tbsps (150 ml) Indian honey

2 tbsps ghee or oil
1 level tsp salt
Pinch of soda bicarb
1 level tsp nigella seeds (kalonji)

Warm water for kneading
Ghee or oil for shallow frying

* Sieve together, flour, salt and soda bicarb.
* Add honey and 2 tbsps of ghee or oil. Mix well. Gradually add warm water and knead well. Knead well and make a pliable dough.
* Divide the dough into 6 equal parts. And shape them into balls.
* Roll out each ball into a disc 5″ (13 cms) diameter. Spread a little ghee or oil on the surface, fold into half and again fold into half. Make a cone. Roll again into a circular disc 5″ (13 cms) diameter. Sprinkle little black nigella seeds on the surface and roll out lightly.
* Heat a griddle, shallow fry one at a time like parathas.

Cooking time: 15 minutes   Makes: 6

87

Bhopali Roti

1½ cups (175 gms) wheat flour
½ cup (50 gms) rice flour
2 tbsps ghee or oil
1 level tsp salt
1 tsp cumin seeds, dry roasted and
ground

3 green chillies, sliced
3 tbsps broken cashewnuts, ground
coarsely
3 tbsps fresh coriander leaves, finely
chopped

6 strands of saffron, soaked
in 2 tbsps warm milk
Water for kneading
Ghee or oil

☆ Sift together wheat flour, rice flour and salt in a bowl. Rub in 2 tbsps of ghee or oil. Add
  rest of the ingredients except oil. Gently add water to make a soft dough. Knead well
  until no longer sticky.
☆ Shape the dough into 8 small balls. On a floured surface, roll out each ball into a
  6″ (15 cms) round.
☆ Heat a griddle. Place the round dough in it and dry roast. When little brown specks
  appear on the underside, turn the roti over. Smear little ghee or oil over the surface and
  drizzle 1 tsp of ghee or oil around the roti. Cook until both the sides are golden brown.
☆ Repeat with the remaining dough.

Cooking time: 30 minutes	Makes: 8

Pakwan

A popular dish of Sind

2 cups (225 gms) plain flour
1 tsp salt

2 tbsps ghee or oil
Pinch of soda bicarb

Water for kneading
Ghee or oil for deep frying

☆ Sieve together flour, salt and soda bicarb. Rub in 2 tbsps ghee or oil.
☆ Add water gradually. Knead well and make a fairly stiff dough.
☆ Divide the dough into 10 equal parts. Shape them into round balls.
☆ Roll out each ball into very thin round disc 6″ (15 cms) diameter. Prick all over with a fork
☆ Heat oil in a frying pan. Deep fry one at a time until golden brown and crisp. Serve hot.

Cooking time: 20 minutes	Makes: 10

Sada Kulcha

Leavened bread of Punjab

4 cups (450 gms) plain flour	1 tsp sugar	3 level tsps dry yeast
4 tbsps (50 gms) yoghurt	½ cup and 2 tbsps (150 ml) warm	2 tbsps poppy seeds
15 gms vegetable oil or ghee	milk or water	1 tsp salt

* Sprinkle sugar and yeast over warm milk and leave it to froth for 20 minutes.
* Sift flour with salt in a bowl. Make a well in the centre. Pour the yeast mixture in it with oil or ghee.
* Mix well and slowly add yoghurt. Knead well. Make a soft dough. Cover with a damp cloth. Leave it to rise **for 6 hours.**
* Knead well again, divide into 10 equal parts. If necessary while kneading add little warm water. Roll out each part into a thick round disc of 5" (13 cms) diameter and ¼" thickness. Place them in a baking tray. Cover with a damp cloth. Leave it to rise again for 30 minutes.
* Brush the top with milk or oil and sprinkle poppy seeds. Bake in a pre-heated oven (140°C-275°F-Gas Mark 1) for 10 minutes. Remove and shallow fry in a hot griddle like parathas.

Variations:

Garlic Kulcha: Grind 2 pods of garlic to a paste. Add little salt and pepper. After dividing the dough into 10 equal parts, make a depression in the centre. Put a little garlic paste and shape into round ball, then roll out. Fry the same way as sada kulcha.

Mint Kulcha: 150 gms mint, 1 tsp sugar, 1 tsp salt, 3 tbsps chopped onion, juice of one lime. Grind all the ingredients together except lime juice and make a paste. Add lime juice. Put 1 tsp of mint paste in each round. Roll out and fry.

Kesari Kulcha: Mix 1 tsp saffron with 2 tbsps milk and 1 tsp sugar. Add this to the dough, while kneading. It enhances the flavour. Roll out and fry.

Panir Kulcha: 175 gms grated cottage cheese. Mix with ½ tsp pepper, ¼ tsp mustard, ½ tsp salt, 1 tsp lime juice. Make a depression in the centre of each portion. Put 2 tsps cheese mixture and shape into round ball. Roll out and fry.

Cooking time: 25 minutes   Makes: 10

Kathi Roll of Nizam

Speciality of Calcutta

3 cups (350 gms) plain flour
2 tsps salt
6 medium size potatoes, boiled,
peeled and mashed

2 tbsps coriander leaves
1 medium onion, finely chopped
1 green chilli, seeded and chopped
Warm water for kneading

2 tbsps ghee or oil
Ghee or oil for shallow frying

☆ Sieve flour and 1 tsp salt in a bowl. Rub in 2 tbsps of ghee or oil.
☆ Gradually add warm water. Mix well. Knead until soft. Place in a well-greased bowl. Cover with a damp cloth. Leave aside for 20 minutes.
☆ Knead again and divide the dough into 9 equal parts. Shape them into round balls. Roll out each into a round disc 7" (18 cms) diameter.
☆ Heat a griddle. Place the roti on dry griddle. Then drizzle 1-2 tsps of ghee or oil around the edges. Do not allow it to become crisp.
☆ Mix together mashed potatoes, 1 tsp salt, onion, chillies and coriander together. Divide into 9 parts.
☆ Stuff each roti with a portion of mashed potatoes. Roll it like a swiss roll. Secure with a cocktail stick.
☆ Cut 9 pieces of butter paper (4" × 4"). Wrap each roll till half way with it. Serve hot with mint chutney.

Note: Instead of potatoes, boiled and mashed eggs, minced meat, or boiled and ground chicken can be used for stuffing.

Cooking time: 35 minutes   Makes: 9   Picture on page: 68

Sweet Warqi Roti

2 cups (225 gms) flour
3 tbsps of castor sugar
225 gms ghee

1 tsp cardamom powder
½ tsp saffron strands
5 tbsps cashewnuts, powdered

2 tbsps raisins, chopped
Few silver warq
Milk for kneading

* Dissolve saffron in 2 tbsps hot milk.
* Sift flour and mix together with sugar, cardamom powder, nuts and raisins.
* Add enough milk in the flour to form a stiff dough.
* Roll the dough into a thick round chapati, cover the surface evenly with ghee, fold and form a triangle, then roll out again into a chapati.
* Repeat the process of folding and rolling out the dough until all the ghee is used up.
* Knead into a smooth dough and with your hand roll out into ¼" thick large circle.
* Cut them into rounds with the help of a biscuit cutter. Place them on a greased baking tray.
* Bake them in pre-heated oven for 30 minutes (140°C-275°F-Gas Mark 1) till golden in colour.
* Spread saffron on top of each and bake for another 2 minutes. Cover with warq.

Cooking time: 50 minutes   Makes: 14   Picture on page: 224

91

Tikkar

Peasant's bread of Malwa

2 cups (225 gms) maize flour
(bhutte ka aata)
2 cups (225 gms) wheat flour
2" ginger, finely chopped

1 onion, grated
10 cloves garlic, crushed
2 tomatoes, seeded and chopped
4 tbsps coriander leaves, chopped
4 tbsps ghee or oil

3 green chillies, deseeded and
chopped
2 tsps salt
Water for kneading
Ghee or oil for shallow frying

* Sift maize flour, wheat flour and salt together in a large bowl. Rub in 4 tbsps ghee or oil.
  Add enough cold water to make a soft dough. Knead well and cover with a damp cloth.
  Keep aside for 20 minutes.
* Gradually knead in all other ingredients except ghee or oil, for shallow frying.
* Divide the dough into 10 equal parts and shape them into round balls.
* Roll them out to a round circle 7" (18 cms) diameter and ½" thickness.
* Cook them on a pre-heated griddle over low heat, one at a time, until brown specks
  appear on both the sides. Then gently add 2-3 tsps of ghee or oil at a time around the
  edges of the roti. Cook until both sides are golden in colour. Serve hot with chutney and
  pickles.

Cooking time: 30 minutes   Makes: 10

Gadai Roti

One of the popular breads of U.P.

4 cups (450 gms) wheat flour
450 gms tender green peas with pods *or*
285 gms dry peas, boiled and coarsely ground

3 green chillies, finely chopped
4 cloves garlic, finely sliced
1 level tsp cumin seeds
1½ level tsp salt

2 tbsps fresh coriander, finely chopped
Water for kneading
Oil for shallow frying

* Sift flour in a bowl, gradually add water and bind the mixture into a soft pliable dough. Knead well for few minutes until the sides of the bowl are clean. Cover with a damp cloth and leave to rest for 15 minutes.
* Wash and boil the pea pods with ½ tsp salt and water to cover. Simmer over medium heat until the pods are tender. Drain and cool. Now shell the peas.
* Mash together the peas, salt, cumin seeds, garlic, green chillies and fresh coriander. Keep aside.
* Knead again the dough. Divide the dough into 10 equal parts. Shape each into a round ball.
* On a floured surface, roll out each to a circle about 3″ (7½ cms) diameter. Place 1 tsp of mashed pea mixture in the centre of the dough and carefully fold up the edges to completely cover up the stuffing. Shape into a ball.
* Dip the stuffed balls into dry flour to prevent sticking while rolling. Roll again into a round of 6″ (15 cms) diameter.
* Heat a griddle. Carefully place the roti on it, one at a time, cook for a minute and turn it over. Smear a little oil on the top and turn it over again. Both sides should have reddish spots, move the roti around so that all ends are exposed to the heat evenly. Remove from heat and serve hot.
* Repeat with remaining dough.

Cooking time: 50 minutes   Makes: 10

Malai Paratha

A delicacy of Punjab

2½ cups (275 gms) wheat flour 1½ level tsps salt Ghee
2 tbsps ghee Water for kneading

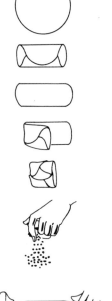

★ Sieve together wheat flour and salt. Rub in 2 tbsps ghee. Add a little water at a time to bind into a soft, pliable dough. Knead for a few minutes until the dough leaves the sides of the bowl absolutely clean. Cover with a damp cloth, leave to rest for 20 minutes.

★ Divide the dough into 9 equal parts. Shape them into round balls. Lightly coat them with dry flour and flatten it slightly on a floured surface. Roll out into a circle of 6″ (15 cms) diameter.

★ Smear enough ghee on top surface. Now carefully fold ⅓ of the circle into the centre and then the other ⅓ over the first fold so that you have a long strip measuring 2″ (5 cms) × 6″ (15 cms). Smear again enough melted ghee on the strip and fold ⅓ of the strip then fold other ⅓ over it so you have a square. Dip this square into dry flour to prevent it from sticking to the rolling surface. Roll out the paratha into a neat square of 5″ × 5″ (13 × 13 cms) and ⅛″ thickness.

★ Heat a griddle or a heavy fry pan. Place the paratha in the centre of the griddle and dry roast for 1-2 seconds. Remove, crush and shape into a ball again. And repeat the stage 3. For each paratha twice dry roast and 6 times, smear it with melted ghee.

★ Now shallow fry the square paratha. Press down the edges with a clean cloth to ensure even cooking. If you want a crisp paratha then smear the top with a little ghee each time you turn or if you want them soft, then wrap them in foil and steam for 15 minutes.

★ Repeat the process with remaining dough. Serve hot.

Cooking time: 1 hour 30 minutes Makes: 9 Picture on page: 10

Coorgi Roti

Snow white rice flour roti of Coorg

cups (225 gms) fine rice flour
½ cups (175 gms) rice, cooked
ery soft

1½ level tsp salt
Water for blending and kneading

Ghee or oil for shallow frying

Sift rice flour and salt together in a bowl.
Put cooked rice with 2 tbsps of water into an electric blender and blend for 1-2 minutes to make a smooth puree.
Mix together rice flour and rice puree, add little water if necessary. Knead to a smooth pliable dough. Divide the dough into 10 equal parts. Shape them into round balls.
Roll out each ball into a round of 6" (15 cms) diameter, 1/6" thickness.
Heat a griddle. Place the round dough in it. Reduce heat and dry roast.
Do not allow the brown specks to appear on the underside, turn the roti over. Press down the edges with a clean piece of cloth to ensure even cooking. Remove from heat and place on a plate.
Repeat with the remaining dough.

ooking time: 30 minutes   Makes: 10

Thepla with Methi

cups (250 gms) wheat flour
cup bajra flour or jowar flour
cup fenugreek leaves, chopped

1 tsp chilli powder
1 tsp coriander powder
1 level tsp salt

½ level tsp turmeric
Oil

Sift together both the flours in a bowl, add fenugreek, salt, coriander powder, chilli powder, turmeric. Add enough water and knead to a smooth dough.
Leave the dough aside for 30 minutes.
Divide into 10 to 15 small balls and roll out to a thin disc.
Heat the griddle and shallow fry like paratha.

ooking time: 30 minutes   Makes: 10-15

Uttapum

South Indian crispy pancake

1 cup (225 gms) basmati rice
100 gms split black gram, without skin
4 green chillies, chopped

1 small onion, grated
2 tbsps coriander, finely chopped
2 tbsps fresh coconut, grated
1 level tsp salt

2 tbsps sour plain yoghurt
1 level tsp soda bicarb
Ghee or oil

* Soak the rice and dal separately **overnight.** Next day wash, drain and grind separately to a smooth paste. This batter should be thick so add very little water while grinding.
* Add yoghurt, soda, beat well until light and frothy. Add onion, chilli, salt, coconut and coriander. Cover and keep aside for 20 minutes.
* Heat griddle or a non-stick pan. Put 1 tsp ghee or oil and pour 2 to 3 tbsps batter. Spread out with back of a soup spoon, into a thick round of 4" (10 cms) diameter. Cook over low heat until small bubbles appear on the surface.
* Turn it over and cook on the other side until crisp and golden. Serve hot with sambar and nariyal chutney.

Cooking time: 30 minutes	Serves: 4-6

Batata Puri

1 cup (100 gms) plain flour
3 tbsps yoghurt
1 tbsp ghee or oil

2 medium size potatoes, boiled, peeled and mashed finely
½ tsp salt

Water for kneading
Ghee or oil for frying

* Mash the potatoes finely. No lumps should remain or the puri will break.
* Sift flour, add salt, yoghurt and mashed potatoes with 1 tbsp of ghee or oil.
* Knead to a soft pliable dough. Divide into 10 round balls. Roll out each into round circles 4" (10 cms) diameter.
* Heat ghee or oil in a heavy pan. Deep fry 1 or 2 puris at a time until the colour turns golden brown.

Cooking time: 15 minutes	Makes: 10

Sada Puri

Plain deep fried puffy bread

cups (225 gms) wheat flour
tbsps melted ghee

1 level tsp salt
Water for kneading

Oil for deep frying

Sift flour and salt in a bowl. Drizzle 2 tbsps melted ghee or oil over the flour and work it in with your fingers till the mixture resembles coarse bread crumbs. Add a little water at a time to form stiff dough. Place the dough over a flat floured surface and knead until smooth and pliable. Cover with a damp cloth for 30 minutes.
Knead the dough again and divide into 20 equal parts. Shape them into round balls, roll out each on a floured surface into a round of 4" to 4½" (10 cms-12 cms) diameter.
Heat oil in a 'karhai' or deep frying pan. To test the temperature of the oil, drop a small piece of dough into it. It should rise to the top at once.
Carefully lift the dough round and slowly put it in the hot oil with the edge of a slotted spoon. Gently push the puri into the hot oil with tiny strokes. It will puff up within seconds, turn it over and cook the other side. Remove the puri with a slotted spoon. Place on a kitchen paper. Serve hot.

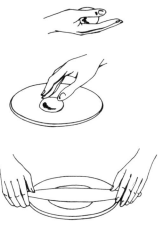

ooking time: 45 minutes   Makes: 20   Picture on page: 67

Indori Palak Puri

A deep fried bread with spinach and spices, Indore (Malwi) style

2 cups (225 gms) wheat flour
2 tbsps ghee or oil
50 gms fresh spinach

1" piece fresh ginger, ground to a
paste
1 level tsp cumin seeds
1 level tsp salt

1 level tsp chilli powder
Water
Ghee or oil for deep frying

* Clean wash and discard the hard stalks of spinach. Boil them with little water until tender. Drain well.
* Sift together flour, salt and chilli powder. Rub in 2 tbsps ghee or oil.
* Add ginger paste, cumin and spinach. Mix thoroughly. Pour little water if necessary. Make a stiff dough.
* Knead the dough for 10 minutes. Cover with a damp cloth and keep aside for 15 minutes.
* Knead again and divide the dough into 20 equal parts and shape into round balls. Roll out into a round disc of 4" (10 cms) diameter. Repeat with rest of the dough.
* Heat oil in a deep frying pan until smoking point. Reduce heat and fry the puris, one at a time.

Cooking time: 25 minutes   Makes: 20   Picture on page: 20

Punjabi Lachha Paratha

2 cups (225 gms) wheat flour
2 tbsps ghee or oil
1 level tsp salt

⅝ cup (150 ml) water
Ghee or oil for shallow frying

⋆ Sieve together flour and salt. Rub in 2 tbsps ghee or oil.
  Slowly add water little at a time. Knead to a smooth and
  pliable dough.
⋆ Divide the dough into 6 equal parts.
⋆ Shape each part into a rope of 14″ (36 cms) in length. Now
  hold in one end and make a coil. Moving your hand in
  clockwise method; spoon a little ghee or oil before placing
  each round.
⋆ Flatten each coil with fingers. Roll out each coil lightly into
  a round disc 5″ (13 cms) diameter.
⋆ Heat a griddle over low heat. Place one paratha at a time,
  drizzle 1-2 spoons ghee or oil around the edges. Shallow
  fry both sides until golden brown.

Cooking time: 30 minutes   Makes: 6

99

Aate ka Pura

Savoury wheat flour pancake of Maharashtra

1 cup (100 gms) wheat flour	4 tbsps fresh coriander leaves, finely	½ level tsp garam masala
1 medium onion, grated	chopped	Water
1 tbsp fresh ginger, finely grated	1 level tsp salt	Ghee or oil
	2 green chillies, seeded and sliced	

* Sift flour and salt in a bowl. Gently add enough water to make a batter of dropping consistency.
* Add rest of the ingredients except oil. Cover and keep aside for 30 minutes.
* Heat a griddle or a non-stick pan. Smear it with a little ghee or oil. Pour 2 tbsps of batter. Spread out with a back of a soup spoon into a thin pancake. As soon as small bubbles appear on the surface, turn it over and drizzle 1 tsp ghee or oil around the pancake. Fry until both the sides are done and turns light golden colour.
* Repeat with the remaining batter. Serve hot.

Variation:

Besan Pura: Use 100 gms gram flour instead of wheat flour. Rest of the ingredients are same.

Cooking time: 35 minutes   Serves: 4-6

Facing Page
Clockwise:

Bermi Roti
Santare ki Lassi
Hari Chutney and Achaa
Fazita
Bafla with Dal
Bathuway ki Roti
Ghassey

Bermi Puri

Jodhpur

1½ cups (175 gms) plain flour	1 level tsp salt
50 gms split green gram, without skin	1 level tsp chilli powder
100 gms spring onions with 4″ stalks, sliced	¼ level tsp cumin seeds
	Water for kneading
	Oil for deep frying

* Clean, wash and soak moong dal **overnight.**
* Next day grind dal together with sliced onion to a fine paste. Add chilli, salt and cumin, grind again 1-2 minutes.
* Sift flour in a bowl. Add all the ground ingredients. Mix well. Add very little water to make a stiff dough. Knead well for 10 minutes until you have a smooth, soft but not sticky dough. Divide the dough into 15 equal balls.
* Flatten one ball at a time. Dust it with some plain flour and roll into a round of 4″ (10 cms) diameter. Bermi puris are little thicker than the usual puris.
* Heat oil in a pan. Let it get very hot. Lift up one puri and lay it carefully over the surface of the hot oil. It will rise in seconds and begin to sizzle. Gently press the centre of the puri down into the oil. This helps the air to distribute evenly and allows the puri to puff up. As soon as the puri rises to the surface, turn it over to cook the other side. Gently press down the edges to ensure thorough and even cooking.

Remove the puri after a few seconds with a slotted spoon. Place on a kitchen paper to drain and keep hot.

Repeat with remaining dough.

Cooking time: 30 minutes	Makes: 15 puris

Facing Page
Clockwise:

Malai Paratha
Chaar

Nargisi Puri

1½ cups (175 gms) plain flour
2 tbsps ghee or oil
2 tsps salt
2 eggs, boiled, peeled and mashed

2 medium potatoes, boiled, peeled and mashed
1 tbsp mint or coriander, finely chopped

1 green chilli, seeded and chopped
Warm water for kneading
Ghee or oil for deep frying

☆ Knead together mashed eggs, potatoes, coriander, chilli and 1 tsp salt and divide into 8 portions.
☆ Sieve flour and 1 tsp salt. Rub in 2 tbsps ghee or oil. Mix well for 10 minutes.
☆ Slowly add warm water. Knead to a soft dough. Divide the dough into 8 equal parts and shape into balls.
☆ Roll out each ball a little. Place one portion of egg mixture in the centre of each round. Fold it over and pinch the ends. Now roll out each into a round puri 4″ (10 cms) diameter Do not make it too thin or the stuffing will come out.
☆ Heat oil in a frying pan, deep fry one at a time until the colour turns golden.
☆ Serve hot with plain yoghurt.

Cooking time: 25 minutes   Makes: 8

Palak ki Puri

2 cups (225 gms) wheat flour
250 gms spinach

1 small onion, chopped
6 tsps milk

1½ tsps salt
Oil for deep frying

☆ Clean and wash spinach. Place in a pan with little water and onion. Cook until tender. Drain and grind to a paste.
☆ Sift flour and salt in a large bowl. Add spinach and milk to make a stiff dough.
☆ Knead the dough well and divide it into 20 parts. Roll them out to round puris 3″ (7.5 cms) diameter.
☆ Heat oil in a deep frying pan. Fry 1 or 2 puris at a time. Turn once. Remove when both sides are cooked.
☆ Serve hot with yoghurt.

Cooking time: 30 minutes   Makes: 20

Mah ki Roti

Madhya Pradesh

2½ cups (275 gms) wheat flour
175 gms sprouted green gram
1 medium onion, grated

1 level tsp chilli powder
2 tbsps fresh coriander leaves, finely chopped

1½ tsps salt
Water for kneading
Ghee or oil

* Sift flour and salt together in a large bowl.
* Combine with chilli powder and onion. Pour a little water at a time, mix well and gather the flour together to form a soft dough. Place on a flat surface, knead to a smooth pliable dough.
* Add sprouted moong dal and coriander leaves. Knead well, for 10-15 minutes. Cover with a damp cloth, keep aside for 30 minutes.
* Knead again and divide the dough into 9 parts. Shape them into round balls.
* Roll out each into a round of 6" (15 cms) diameter. Sprinkle little flour on the rolling surface if it is sticky.
* Heat a griddle and dry roast the roti on both sides.
* Drizzle 1 tbsp of ghee or oil over the roti and another spoon around its edges. Turn it over and cook until both the sides are golden brown.
* Repeat with remaining dough.
* Serve hot.

Cooking time: 50 minutes   Makes: 9   Picture on page: 206

Koki (Plain)

Sind

2 cups (225 gms) wheat flour	½ tsp pepper	Lukewarm water
1 tsp salt	4 tbsps ghee or oil	

* Sift wheat flour and salt together in a bowl, add pepper. Rub in ghee or oil. Gradually add water. Mix well and knead to a smooth dough.
* Divide the dough into 8 parts. Shape them into round balls. Roll each ball out into a round disc about 3" (7.5 cms) diameter.
* Heat the griddle. Bake both the sides of the disc for 2-3 seconds. Remove from heat and roll out again into a round disc 5" (12 cms) diameter.
* Place it back to the griddle and spoon ghee or oil round the edges. Cook until both sides are golden brown in colour. Remove and serve hot with sai bhaji.

Cooking time: 30 minutes　　　　　　　　Makes: 8

Masala Koki

1 cup (100 gms) gram flour (besan)	1 tsp coriander powder	1 medium onion, grated
½ cup (50 gms) wheat flour	2 tbsps coriander leaves, chopped	Cold water
2 green chillies (optional)	finely	Ghee or oil
2 tbsps ghee or oil	1 tsp salt	
	6 cloves garlic, crushed	

* Sift gram flour, wheat flour and salt in a bowl. Rub in 2 tbsps ghee or oil. Gradually add water. Knead to a smooth dough.
* Add coriander powder, chillies, coriander leaves, garlic and onion. Knead well.
* Proceed as plain Koki (see above). Follow the directions carefully.
* Serve masala Koki with any raita or plain yoghurt.

Cooking time: 30 minutes　　　　　　　　Makes: 8

Dhohdha

Barley flour bread (A Sindhi speciality)

2 cups (225 gms) barley flour (jowar aata)
1 tsp salt
1 medium onion, finely chopped

1 green chilli, finely chopped
2 tbsps coriander leaves, chopped
3 tbsps lime juice
Ghee for shallow frying

Cold water for kneading
Little extra flour

* Sift flour and salt together. Gradually add cold water and knead to a very soft dough. Cover with a damp cloth. Keep aside for 20 minutes.
* Knead again. Add chopped chilli, coriander leaves, onion and lime juice. Knead again.
* Divide the dough into 10 equal parts.
* Wet your hands with cold water. Now take one part of the dough, keep between your palms, pat and press alternately shifting it from one palm to another. Make a round disc, like a chapati, 6″ diameter.
* Heat a griddle and put a tsp of ghee. Sprinkle little cold water over the griddle and place the Dhohdha on it. Little ghee can be added if necessary. Turn and cook both the sides until brown. Make one at a time and serve with pickle, chutney or vegetable.

Cooking time: 30 minutes   Makes: 10   Picture on page: 33

Baroda Dal Dhokli

Baroda style

For dhokli
1 cup (100 gms) wheat flour
½ tsp turmeric
½ tsp chilli powder
Water for mixing
2 tsps oil
1 tsp salt

For dal
1 cup (160 gms) red gram (tuvar dal)
5 cups (1.25 lt) water
2 tsps sugar
1 medium onion, sliced
1 level tsp aamchur
2 level tsps salt
½ tsp garam masala
1 tsp turmeric

For tadka
2 tbsps ghee or oil
3 flakes garlic, crushed
10 kadi patta
½ tsp cumin seeds
2 tsps red chilli powder
½ tsp mustard seeds
A pinch of asafoetida

* Put dal with water in a heavy pan and boil over high heat. Add onion, turmeric powder and sugar. Remove scum if any from top.
* Sift flour, add salt and the spices. Rub in oil and slowly add water. Make a stiff dough. Knead well until smooth.
* Divide dough into 4 to 5 balls. Roll out each into a rectangle as thick as a chapati. Cut each rolled out piece with a sharp knife into small squares 2″ × 2″ pieces.
* Mix dal thoroughly with wooden spoon and strain. Add salt and place over a low flame. Drop cut pieces of dhoklis into the boiling dal. Cook until done. Remove and sprinkle garam masala and aamchur.
* Heat oil in a separate pan. Put curry leaves, mustard seeds, cumin seeds, garlic, chilli powder and asafoetida. Pour onto the dal dhokli. Remove from heat after 2 minutes.
* Put in a bowl. Garnish with coriander leaves. This is a complete meal. Rotis are not served with dhokli. Serve with melted ghee and onion-tomato kachumber.

Cooking time: 30 minutes   Makes: 6   Picture on page: 15:

Aluwala Roti

Punjab

2 cups (225 gms) wheat flour
1 level tsp salt
Water for mixing
Ghee or oil for shallow frying

For filling
4 medium potatoes
1 small onion, grated
1 tsp salt
½ tsp pepper
1 tsp coriander leaves, chopped

* Sift wheat flour with salt. Slowly add water. Mix well. Make a stiff dough. Cover with a damp cloth for 20 minutes.
* Boil potatoes, peel and mash. Add salt, onion, pepper and coriander. Mix well. Divide into 8 portions.
* Knead dough well until smooth and pliable. Divide into 6 round balls. Flatten each ball slightly. Put one portion of filling in the centre. Close up carefully. Shape into round balls again.
* Roll out each ball on a lightly floured board into a round disc 6" (15 cms) diameter.
* Cook one at a time on a hot griddle over medium heat. Put about 1 or 2 tbsps ghee around the edge. Turn gently. Cook until both the sides turns golden brown in colour. Serve with yoghurt.

Vegetarian Kheema Roti: Instead of potato stuffing, use cooked and seasoned vegetarian minced meat for stuffing. Serve with plain yoghurt.

Cooking time: 20 minutes   Makes: 6   Picture on page: 153

Paneer ki Roti

Cottage cheese bread

2 cups (225 gms) wheat flour
1 cup (125 gms) cottage cheese or
paneer, mashed (see page 17)

2 level tsps salt
2 tbsps ghee
½ tsp cumin seeds, crushed

1 tbsp coriander leaves,
chopped finely
Water for kneading
Ghee for shallow frying

☆ Sift wheat flour, 1 tsp salt together in a bowl. Combine well with 2 tbsps ghee, cumin seeds. Add water and knead to a soft dough. Cover with a damp cloth leave aside for 20 minutes.

☆ To prepare the filling, rub cottage cheese through a sieve. Mix well with 1 tsp salt and coriander leaves. Divide into 6 equal parts and roll them into balls.

☆ Knead the dough again, divide into 6 portions, and shape them into flat rounds.

☆ Roll each round into size of a puri, place one cheese ball in the centre of each roti and bring all sides together and cover and form a flattened round.

☆ Now roll out each ball into circle of 5″ (12 cms) diameter.

☆ Cook them like plain parathas in a hot griddle, smear with ghee.

☆ Serve cheese roti with any dish of vegetable or chutney.

Cooking time: 30 minutes   Makes: 6

Masala Baati

1½ cups (175 gms) coarse wheat flour
½ cup (50 gms) gram flour (besan)
4 tbsps hot ghee

3 tbsps onion, finely chopped
1 tsp salt
½ tsp cumin seeds

3 cloves of garlic, crushed
Water for kneading
Ghee for serving

* Sift both the flours together. Add all the ingredients.
* Add just enough water to make a stiff dough, knead well.
* Divide into 6 equal parts and shape them into round balls. Make a depression in the centre of each baati.
* Place baatis in a baking tray.
* Bake in a pre-heated oven (220°C-425°F-Gas Mark 7) for 15-20 minutes. If using a tandoor, place it over high flame for 15-20 minutes.
* When baked, press each baked baati into the hot ghee and then serve.
* Serve hot with dal or kadhi. Also can be served with any meat or vegetable gravy.

Note: If you want to serve baati in the traditional style, then heat ghee in a pan, press each cooked baati one at a time in ghee. It should break up into 1 to 4 parts. Remove at once from ghee and serve.

Cooking time: 20 minutes   Makes: 6

Kashmiri Puri

1 cup (100 gms) plain flour	1 tsp dry yeast	8 strands of saffron or pinch of
1 cup (100 gms) wheat flour	5/8 cup (150 ml) warm milk	jalebi colour
½ tsp salt	2 tbsps sugar	1 tsp poppy seeds
1 tbsp aniseeds, roasted and ground	2 tbsps yoghurt	Ghee for deep frying

* Sprinkle yeast and 1 tsp sugar over the warm milk. Cover and leave aside for 30 minutes.
* Sift together wheat flour, plain flour and salt in a bowl. Add remaining sugar and aniseeds. Gradually pour in yeast liquid mix and knead well for 15-20 minutes until dough becomes soft and smooth. Cover with a damp cloth. Leave it aside for **4 to 6 hours.** But for best result leave it **overnight** in a warm place.
* Next morning knead again. Divide the dough into 20 portions. Shape them into round balls.
* Roll out each ball on a floured board into a round puri 4" (10 cms) diameter.
* Mix well saffron, yoghurt and poppy seeds together. Leave aside for 15 minutes.
* Smear one side of each puri with saffron mixture before frying.
* Heat ghee or oil in a deep frying pan and fry 1 or 2 puris at a time until it turns golden brown.
* Serve hot with Kashmiri Dahi (see page 222).

Cooking time: 45 minutes   Makes: 20

Taihdar Roti

Layered roti

4 cups (450 gms) wheat flour
2 tbsps ghee
2 cups (225 gms) vegetarian minced meat, washed and cleaned (see page 18)

1 small onion, finely chopped
1 tsp coriander powder
½ tsp chilli powder
1 tsp garam masala

1 tbsp lemon juice
Ghee or oil
Lukewarm water

* Sift wheat flour with salt. Add 1 tbsp ghee, mix well with fingertips. Add enough water. Knead well. Make a smooth dough. Cover with a damp muslin. Leave aside for 30 minutes.
* Heat 2 tbsps ghee or oil. Saute onion till brown in colour. Add coriander, chilli powder, garam masala, salt and minced meat or soya nuggets. Fry until brown. Add ½ cup water. Cover and let it simmer until tender. Add more water if necessary but the mince must be dry when done.
* Knead the dough again. Divide into 24 parts. You will require 8 balls for 1 roti.
* Roll out first four balls, each separately, into thin chapatis. Smear one with ghee then place another on it, now again smear the top with ghee and place another, until you have layer of four.
* Sprinkle lemon juice over cooked minced meat mix well. Divide this into 3 parts. Sprinkle the top of the chapati with little water then spread a thin layer of mince. Cover with 4 more chapatis smeared well with ghee before placing each one. Roll the roti a little or press with finger.
* Cook on a hot griddle one at a time. Add a little ghee on the sides of the roti. Fry until both sides are golden brown and crisp.
* Serve hot with any of the raitas or vegetable dishes.

| Cooking time: 55 minutes | Makes: 3 | Picture on page: 224 |

Mysore Idli

South India

1 cup (225 gms) rice	2 tsps salt	2 tbsps oil
¾ (100 gms) split black gram	15 gms cashewnuts, chopped finely and roasted	

☆ Soak dal and rice **overnight** in separate containers.

☆ Next day grind rice with little water. Make a thick paste.

☆ Grind the dal separately with little water. Make a smooth paste. Mix both the paste together, add salt. Leave it **again overnight** to ferment.

☆ Next day beat well and put 1 or 2 tbsps to each lightly oiled idli mould, or pour in greased small cake tins, sprinkle cashewnuts and steam for 15 minutes. Serve with sambar and nariyal chutney.

Variations:

Dal Idli: Take 100 gms black split gram and 100 gms moong dal instead of rice. Add ½" piece ground ginger. Proceed as Mysore Idli.

Coconut Idli: Take one recipe Mysore Idli, add 25 gms grated coconut. Proceed as above.

Kanchipuram Idli: This special idli is prepared at the Vaishnavite temple of Sri Devraja Swamy in Kanchipura. Idlis are steamed in larger moulds. Each idli weighs about 3 pounds. It is cut into small slices and offered to the devotees. This cannot be made at home.

Cooking time: 15 minutes   Makes: 22   Picture on page: 119

Dum ki Roti

2 cups (225 gms) wheat flour
2 tsps salt
Pinch of soda bicarb

2 tbsps onions, chopped
⅝ cup (150 ml) cold water
10 tbsps coconut, grated

Ghee or oil for shallow frying
(optional)

* Sift wheat flour in a bowl. Add salt, onion and soda. Pour all water at once. Mix briskly with a wooden spoon. Cover and keep aside **for 1 hour.**
* Beat well for 2 minutes and make a thick batter of pouring consistency.
* Heat the griddle. Grease lightly, pour ½ cup of batter on it. Spread lightly with back of spoon. Sprinkle 1 tbsp coconut on each roti.
* Cover and cook for 1 or 2 minutes over medium heat, until light brown in colour. Remove the lid, turn at once and brown the other side. If needed, put little more ghee or oil around the edges.
* Repeat same with the rest of batter. Keep warm. For re-heating wrap them in foil and place them in moderately hot oven for 10 minutes. Serve with raita.

Cooking time: 20 minutes	Makes: 10

Hari Roti

Pea roti

2 cups (225 gms) whole wheat flour
1½ cups (150 gms) peas, shelled,
boiled and mashed

2 level tsps salt
2 tbsps lime juice
1 cup mint or coriander leaves,
chopped

2 tbsps ghee or oil
½ tsp pepper
Water for kneading
Ghee or oil for shallow frying

* Sift wheat flour with salt. Rub in 2 tbsps ghee or oil. Add mashed peas. Mix thoroughly.
* Add pepper, coriander or mint with lime juice. Knead well. Divide into 8 equal portions. Shape them into round balls.
* Roll each ball on a floured board into circle 5″ (12 cms) diameter.
* Lift each roti carefully with floured hands. Place on a hot griddle one at a time. Shallow fry with 1 or 2 tbsps ghee or oil until both the sides well cooked.

Cooking time: 25 minutes	Makes: 8	Picture on page: 205

Bafla with Dal

Rajasthani bread

For bafla
2 cups (225 gms) wheat flour
4 tbsps ghee or oil
1 tsp salt
Water for kneading
Extra ghee or oil

For dal
225 gms split green gram
(moong dal)
5½ cups (1.25 lt) water
1 tsp turmeric powder
2 tsps salt
1 tsp sugar

2 medium onions, chopped
2 green chillies
2 bay leaves
2 (2″) cinnamon sticks
3 tbsps oil
2 tbsps coriander, chopped

☆ Put moong dal with water in a heavy pan over high heat. Add half of the chopped onion, salt, turmeric, sugar, green chillies, bay leaves, cinnamon sticks.

☆ Sift flour with salt, rub in ghee or oil. Knead to a smooth dough.

☆ Divide the dough into 10 parts and shape them into round balls.

☆ Drop these flour balls into the boiling dal, reduce heat. Cook for 25 minutes then remove the cooked flour balls one by one from the dal.

☆ Place the cooked flour balls in a greased baking dish. Bake in a pre-heated oven (375°F-190°C-Gas Mark 5) until the skin of baflas begins to crack and colour turns light brown.

☆ Place them in a dish and press each of them in the centre with your thumb. Break lightly and put 1 or 2 tsps ghee into each bafla. Can be eaten without ghee too.

☆ Heat 3 tbsps oil in a pan. Fry remaining half of onions until lightly browned. Pour cooked dal. Stir well. Let it boil 2-3 times. Remove from fire and sprinkle chopped coriander.

☆ Serve baflas with dal.

Note: Dal should be poured over the baflas, breaking them completely. Other vegetable dishes or chutney can be served with it also.

Cooking time: 35 minutes   Makes: 10   Picture on page: 101

116

Dahi Luchi

Soft and delicious

2 cups (225 gms) plain flour
⅝ cup (150 ml) plain yoghurt

2 tbsps ghee
½ tsp salt

Ghee or oil for deep frying

* ☆ Sift flour and salt in a bowl.
* ☆ Add yoghurt and mix well. Gradually add ghee little at a time.
* ☆ Knead well, make a stiff dough. If dough is too stiff sprinkle little warm water. Cover and leave to stand for 15 minutes.
* ☆ Knead for 2 minutes again and divide dough into 15 equal size round balls.
* ☆ Roll out each into round circle 3″ (7.5 cms) diameter.
* ☆ Heat ghee or oil in a heavy pan (about 2½″ high), fry 1 or 2 luchis at a time until colour turns golden brown on both sides. Serve hot.

Cooking time: 30 minutes	Makes: 15	Picture on page: 223

Roghni Roti

Milk bread

2 cups (225 gms) wheat flour *or*
1 cup wheat flour with 1 cup plain flour

3 tbsps melted butter or cream
½ level tsp salt
⅝ cup (150 ml) warm milk

Ghee or oil for shallow frying
6 strands of saffron, soaked in
2 tbsps milk

* ☆ Sift flour and salt in a bowl. Rub in melted butter or cream. Gently add enough warm milk to make soft dough and knead well until no longer sticky. Cover and keep aside for 20 minutes.
* ☆ Knead again and divide into 8 portions and shape them into round balls.
* ☆ On a floured surface, roll each ball into a round of 6″ (15 cms) diameter.
* ☆ Brush the top of each roti with saffron solution.
* ☆ Heat a griddle. Shallow fry the roti until both the sides turn golden brown. Turn over and cook 1-2 minutes and remove from fire. Cook and store as parathas. Repeat with remaining dough.

Cooking time: 30 minutes	Makes: 8

Suji (Semolina) Idli

South Indian steamed bread

1 cup and 1 level tbsp (150 gms) semolina (suji)
1 cup (250 gms) yoghurt
1 tsp mustard seeds

Pinch of soda bicarb
½ tsp baking powder
15 gms cashewnuts, chopped finely
1 tbsp black gram dal

1 tsp salt
2 dry chillies, chopped (optional)
Ghee or oil for frying
Water for mixing

* Sieve semolina in a bowl. Blend well with salt, soda bicarb, baking powder and yoghurt. Leave to stand for 30 minutes.
* Heat 2 tbsps ghee or oil, fry dal, cashewnuts and mustard seeds with dry red chillies. Remove as the colour changes. Add to the semolina mixture. Add little water to make a thick idli batter.
* Put 1 or 2 tbsps on each idli mould. If you do not have idli mould, then put in Ramkin dishes, cover and steam for 15 minutes. Test with a fork. If the idli is cooked it will come out clean. Serve hot with sambar and chutney.

Cooking time: 45 minutes   Makes: 22

Facing Page
Clockwise:

Dahi ka Shorba
Sambhar
Nariyal ki Chutney
Kaju ki Kari
Masala Dosa
Idlis

Laal Roti
Beetroot Roti

½ cups (175 gms) wheat flour
medium beetroot, finely grated
tsps vegetable oil or ghee
tsp salt

1 tsp pepper
1 tsp cardamom powder
Vegetable oil or ghee for shallow
frying

Extra flour
Water for kneading

Sift wheat flour in a bowl. Add salt, 2 tsps oil or ghee, cardamom powder, pepper and grated beetroot, mix well. Add water knead to a smooth dough.
Divide the dough into 9 equal portions, shape them into round balls.
Flatten and roll out each ball into disc of 5″ (12 cms) diameter. Dust with extra flour.
Heat a griddle on a slow fire. Cook one at a time, using 2 or 3 tsps oil or ghee. Shallow fry the rotis turning once or twice until both the sides are cooked and turn lightly brown.

Variation:

Mitha Laal Roti: Take same ingredients as recipe of Laal roti. Add 50 gms castor sugar or grated jaggery before kneading with water and proceed the same way as directed. Children ove this roti.

ooking time: 30 minutes	Makes: 9	Picture on page: 205

acing Page
ockwise:

ashmiri Methi Chaman
akkai ki Roti
nefre
adkewali Dal
onkan Murgh
agaru Pudina ka Dahi (centre)

Punjabi Cheela

Savoury Indian green gram pancake

1 cup (100 gms) green gram, without skins
½ cup (60 gms) peas, shelled
4 cloves garlic, chopped
1" piece fresh ginger, sliced

4 green chillies, seeded and chopped
1 cup spring onions, chopped
½ level tsp turmeric powder
¼ level tsp soda bicarb
1½ level tsps salt

1 level tsp chilli powder
2 tbsps fresh coriander leaves finely chopped
4 tbsps water
Butter or oil

★ Wash and soak dal **overnight.** Next day drain and keep aside.

★ Soak peas in boiling water for 10 minutes and drain. Grind coarsely.

★ Combine together the dal, onion, garlic, ginger, chillies, turmeric, salt, chilli powder and grind to a smooth paste with 4 tbsps water.

★ Put the batter into a bowl. Add coriander leaves and peas. Mix well and keep in a refrigerator **for 5 hours,** for better result keep it **for 24 hours.**

★ Add soda bicarb just before cooking and stir well.

★ Heat a non-stick pan or griddle. Put in 1 tbsp butter or oil. As soon as the oil heats, pour in 2 tbsps batter. Now using a round bottom spoon gently spread the batter outward with the back of the spoon in a continuous spiral motion. Make a round pancake of 5"-6" (12-15 cms) diameter.

★ Drizzle a tsp of oil over the pancake and another spoon around its edges. Cover and cook over medium heat for 1-2 minutes, then turn it over and cook for another 1 minute until both the sides of the pancake turn golden brown and crisp. Repeat with remaining batter.

★ Remove from heat and place in a plate and cover. Or stock them on a sheet of aluminium foil, then wrap them into a bundle.

★ Cheelas are best eaten hot. Also the whole bundle can be reheated in an oven (425° F-220°C-Gas Mark 7) for 10 minutes.

Cooking time: 30 minutes	Makes: 15-18

Methi Puri

North India

1 cup (100 gms) wheat flour	3 tbsps coriander leaves, finely cut	Water
1 cup fenugreek leaves, finely cut	Pinch of turmeric powder	Ghee to fry

* Sift flour in a bowl and mix rest of the ingredients with 1 tsp ghee.
* Make a soft dough using water, knead well for 15-20 minutes.
* Divide the dough into 20 portions. Shape them into round balls.
* Roll out each ball on a floured board into a round puri 4" (10 cms) diameter.
* Heat ghee in a deep frying pan and fry 1 or 2 puris at a time until it turns golden brown.
* Serve hot with raita and a vegetable dish.

Cooking time: 40 minutes   Makes: 20   Picture on page: 154

Missie Roti

1 cup (100 gms) wheat flour or corn flour	1 tsp salt	Ghee to fry
1 cup (100 gms) bengal gram flour	1 tsp cumin seeds, roasted and ground	Water
2 cups spinach, finely cut	1 medium onion, grated	

* Sift both the flours together in a bowl. Add salt, spinach, onion and cumin seeds.
* Add enough water and knead to a smooth pliable dough.
* Divide the dough into 6 equal parts and roll each into a round ball.
* Roll out each round a floured surface, rub ghee on top. Now cut into 4 parts lengthways, then place the cut pieces on top of the centre one. It will make one long strip. Now roll it like a swiss roll, press and flatten it with your fingers.
* Slowly roll out to a square 4" × 4".
* Fry on a griddle on medium flame, drizzling a little ghee on each side.
* Serve hot with vegetable and meat dish.

Cooking time: 30 minutes   Makes: 6

Dhansakh

A classic parsi dish traditionally cooked with meat, mixed dals and vegetables

½ cup (100 gms) red gram (tuvar dal)
½ cup (100 gms) red split lentil (masoor dal)
1 small aubergine, peeled and cubed
3″ piece yellow pumpkin, peeled and cubed
1 bunch small coriander, chopped
1 bunch small methi or spinach leaves, chopped
2 large tomatoes, chopped
2 medium onions, sliced
1 tsp tamarind pulp
1 level tsp turmeric powder

1 tsp grated jaggery
½ tsp chilli powder
4 tbsps melted ghee or oil
2 level tsps salt
2 level tsps dhania-zeera powder (omit if using dhansakh masala)

Ground to a paste
1 full pod of garlic
4″ piece of fresh ginger
6 dry Kashmiri chillies
1½ tsps cumin seeds
1½ tsps coriander seeds
6 peppercorns

2″ cinnamon stick
3 cardamoms, peeled
3-4 cloves
or you may use
2 tsps dhansakh masala
2 tsps sambhar masala (available in grocery stores)
7 cloves garlic, 1 × 1″ piece fresh ginger, ground to a paste

For garnishing
2 onions sliced and fried
2 tsps coriander leaves, finely chopped
2 green chillies, slit lengthways

☆ Heat ghee or oil in a heavy bottom pan, fry onion until brown. Stir in masala paste with dhania-zeera and turmeric powder. Stir well and cook for a few minutes.
☆ Boil dals, vegetables and chopped herbs. Mash and strain the mixture. Add to the sauted masalas.
☆ Pour in water, add salt. Bring to the boil, cover and reduce heat. Cook until done.
☆ Add jaggery. Mix well and cook over low heat for 15 minutes. Garnish with fried onions, coriander and chillies.
☆ Serve hot, with brown rice.

Note: This recipe tastes excellent with meat. The meat should be added to the sauted masala and cooked till tender. Then add the dals and vegetables.

Cooking time: 30 minutes	To serve: 4-6	Picture on page: 172

Dal Maharani

Punjabi black dal with kidney beans

2 cups (300 gms) whole black lentils
½ cup (100 gms) red kidney beans,
(rajmah) **soaked overnight**
5½ cups (1.25 lt) cold water
1½ cups (575 ml) milk
2 large onions, 8 cloves garlic and
1½" piece ginger, finely chopped

2 dry red Kashmiri chillies
1 level tsp garam masala
2 level tsps salt
4 tbsps ghee, melted
2 bay leaves

4 tbsps o.
3 green chii.
lengthways
2 tbsps cream o. ...ite butter
2 tbsps chopped coriander
leaves

* Clean and wash black dal. Add water, kidney beans and half of the chopped ingredients. Simmer over low heat until the dal and beans are soft. Add ghee.
* Add milk, stir well, cook gently. Add little more water if necessary. Mash the dal with a wooden spoon. Simmer again until it acquires a creamy consistency and add salt. Remove from heat.
* Heat oil, fry bay leaves and dry red chillies. Add remaining chopped onion, garam masala, garlic and ginger. Fry until lightly brown and add cooked dal. Mix well, remove from heat.
* Add cream just before serving. Garnish with green chillies and chopped coriander leaves.

Cooking time: 4-5 hours	To serve: 6	Picture on page: 154

Haleem Qutub Shahi

A royal dish from Hyderabad. Vegetables are cooked
with wheat, lentils and spices

1½ cups broken wheat
4 tbsps red gram (tuvar dal)
2 tbsps lentil (masoor dal)
2 tbsps split Bengal gram (chana dal)
100 gms cauliflower, peas and
brinjals, cut into pieces
2 capsicums, cut
3 medium onions, sliced

8 cloves garlic, and 2 tbsps grated
fresh ginger, ground to a paste
1 tsp turmeric powder
1 tsp chilli powder
1 tbsp garam masala (see page 19)
1 tbsp coriander seeds and 1 tbsp
cumin seeds, ground to a fine paste

2 level tsps salt
6 cups (1½ lt) water
8 tbsps ghee or oil

For garnishing
1 onion, sliced and fried
1 tbsp coriander leaves,
chopped

* Soak wheat and dals separately **overnight**. Wash well to remove the husks and outer skin. Drain and keep aside for 20 minutes.
* Heat half the melted ghee or oil. Fry onions until brown. Stir in garlic, ginger paste, fry for a few minutes. Add coriander-cumin paste, turmeric, chilli, salt and add wheat and dal mixture. Stir well.
* Pour in water. Cover and cook slowly over low heat for 1 hour until wheat grains are soft and pulpy and dals are tender. Add vegetables. Stir well. When ready add garam masala and remaining ghee or oil. Keep stirring. Cook over low heat without cover until ghee floats to the top and colour turns golden.
* Pour into a serving bowl or a deep dish. Sprinkle fried onions and coriander on top. Serve hot with lemon slices, mint leaves and kachumber.

Cooking time: 1½ hours   To serve: 4-6

Sambar

South Indian

2 cups (330 gms) red gram (tuvar dal)
2 tsps chick peas
4 dry red Kashmiri chillies
1 tsp coriander seeds
4 tbsps freshly grated coconut
A pinch of asafoetida

8 curry leaves
1 tsp mustard seeds
¼ tsp fenugreek seeds, coarsely powdered
½ tsp turmeric powder

For vegetables
6 small onions (size of a marble)
1 medium size aubergine, cut into cubes
1 tender drumstick, cut into 2″ pieces
6 tender okras, whole
6 french beans, cleaned and cut into 2 pieces
65 gms tamarind, soaked in 1 cup water
8 cups (2 lt) water
2 tbsps oil

- Heat 1 tbsp oil and fry chick peas, red chillies, coriander seeds and asafoetida in a frying pan till crisp. Add the grated coconut and roast these ingredients for a minute. Then grind them together to a smooth paste.
- Squeeze tamarind pods in a bowl. The remaining rub through a sieve. Keep the pulp aside and discard seeds and fibres.
- Cook red gram in boiling water with turmeric powder, cook until the gram is soft. Remove from heat.
- Heat remaining oil, fry mustard and fenugreek seeds till they splutter. Add cut vegetables and saute for 2 minutes.
- Mix tamarind extract, salt and ground paste with 5 tbsps water and add to the vegetables. Cook over low heat stirring occasionally for 7-8 minutes.
  Add cooked red gram and simmer for about 15 minutes, until well mixed.
  Serve hot with idlis or rice.

Cooking time: 45 minutes | To serve: 4-6 | Picture on page: 119

Mangalorean Sprouted Mung Curry

200 gms sprouted green gram
2 green chillies
2½ cups (575 ml) water
A pinch of asafoetida
3 tbsps oil
10 curry leaves
1½ tsps salt
1 tsp cumin seeds

Ground to a paste
½ fresh coconut, grated
1 tsp roasted coriander seeds
4 bedgi chillies, roasted (see page 24)
¼ tsp turmeric powder
5 tbsps tamarind pulp

* Wash sprouted mung carefully. Pour enough water to cover the sprouts and add chillies. Cook gently over low heat until tender.
* Add the ground masala and salt. Mix well. Simmer over low heat until done.
* Heat oil. Add cumin seeds and when they splutter, add asafoetida and curry leaves. Pour over the boiled sprouts. Mix well. Serve hot.

Cooking time: 1 hour   To serve: 4-6

Chole Pindi

Savoury chick peas of Punjab

175 gms chick peas or Kabuli chana, cleaned and washed
2 medium onions, finely chopped
1 medium tomato, chopped
Pinch of soda bicarb
2 tsps garlic, chopped
2 tsps ginger, chopped

½ tsp turmeric powder
1 tsp garam masala (see page 19)
½ tsp coriander powder
1 level tsp cumin seeds, roasted and powdered
3 tbsps tamarind pulp (see page 20)

1 green chilli, seeded and chopped
2 level tsps salt
2 tbsps mint or coriander leaves, finely chopped
2 bay leaves
4 tbsps oil
2 cups (425 ml) water

☆ Dissolve soda bicarb in 425 ml water and soak the chick peas **overnight.**
☆ Cook chick peas with water in a pressure cooker for 45 minutes until chick peas are soft.
☆ Heat oil, fry onion, bay leaves, garlic, ginger, turmeric powder, coriander powder, green chilli and fry till brown.
☆ Add chopped tomatoes and cook for 2-3 minutes.
☆ Pour soaked chick peas, salt, garam masala, cumin seeds powder and tamarind pulp. Mix well and cook for 10-15 minutes.
☆ Serve hot. Garnish with coriander leaves, onion rings, sliced tomatoes and lemons.

Cooking time: 1 hour 10 minutes   To serve: 4-6

Dal Palak

Moong dal and spinach seasoned with spice.
All time favourite of North Indians.

450 gms fresh spinach, washed and chopped
175 gms split green gram, cleaned and washed
3¾ cups (900 ml) water
1 tsp fresh ginger, grated
1½ level tsps salt
6 cloves garlic, crushed

For tadka
3 tsps oil
3 tomatoes, chopped
2 green chillies, seeded and chopped
1 level tsp cumin seeds
2 medium onions, chopped

☆ Clean and wash the spinach, discarding yellow leaves. Chop roughly.
☆ Place moong dal and spinach together with water in a pan. Simmer over low heat.
☆ Add garlic, ginger and salt. Stir well. Cook until dal becomes very soft and spinach blends well.
☆ To prepare tadka, heat oil and fry cumin seeds. As they splutter add onion, stir well and fry until brown. Add tomatoes, green chillies, fry for a few minutes more. Pour over the dal and mix well. Serve hot.

Cooking time: 30 minutes   To serve: 4-6

Dhingri Chole

Dry white Kashmiri mushrooms with potatoes and oriental spices

5 gms large mushrooms
5 gms whole white chick peas
aked **overnight**
medium onions or 4 spring onions
cloves garlic, crushed

2 level tsps curry powder
1 level tsp garam masala
1 tsp lemon juice
1 tsp cumin seeds, 1 tsp coriander
seeds, 1 tsp grated fresh ginger,
ground to a paste.

3 large tomatoes, chopped
1 level tsp turmeric powder
1½ level tsps salt
3 tsps melted ghee or oil
2 tsps fresh coriander leaves,
finely chopped

Soak mushrooms and chick peas separately **overnight**. Next day wash mushrooms and
thoroughly discard the woody stalks.
Cut them into small 1″ × 1″ pieces. Boil until soft. Drain and keep aside.
Heat ghee or oil over medium heat, fry onion until brown, add garlic and ground paste
and fry for few minutes until colour turns light golden. Add tomatoes and stir well. Fry
until oil begins to separate.
Add chick peas with mushrooms. Mix well, stir and fry for 10 minutes. Add water.
Increase heat and bring to a boil. Reduce heat and cover. Simmer until chick peas are
tender.
Garnish with coriander leaves. Serve hot.

oking time: 30 minutes
To serve: 4-6
Picture on page: 67

131

Sabat Moong Dal

1 cup (160 gms) whole green gram
6 cloves garlic, sliced
5 tbsps fresh ginger, grated
1 level tsp ground turmeric
1½ level tsps salt

11 cups (1.3 lt) water
3 tbsps fresh coriander, chopped
2 green chillies, seeded and slit
lengthways

For tadka
3 tbsps melted ghee or oil
2 dry Kashmiri chillies, broken
into small pieces
1 level tsp cumin seeds
2 medium tomatoes

☆ Clean and soak dal **for 4 hours**.
☆ Drain and wash. Place together with half of the water. Bring rapidly to boil over high heat
☆ Add ginger, garlic, turmeric and salt. Reduce heat. Cover. Simmer over low heat, until green grams become soft. Add rest of the water.
☆ To prepare the tadka, heat ghee or oil, add cumin seeds and as they splutter add chillies and tomatoes. Stir, fry 4-5 minutes.
☆ Pour this over the cooked dal. Stir well.
☆ Garnish with coriander leaves and green chillies before serving.

Cooking time: 1 hour   To serve: 4-6

Calcutta Ghugni

*A classic festival dish of Bengal. Chick peas
cooked with coconut and oriental spices*

½ cups (225 gms) white chick peas
level tsp soda bicarb
fresh coconut, cut into thin strips
nd then sliced finely
large onions, sliced
fresh ginger and 8 cloves garlic,
ound to a paste
tsp cumin seeds
big cardamoms

2 tsps coriander seeds and 1½ tsps
cumin seeds, ground to a paste
8 small green cardamoms, 8 cloves
and 4 1½″ length pieces cinnamon,
dry ground together
1 large potato, peeled and diced

5 tbsps plain yoghurt
3 level tsps granulated sugar
1 level tsp turmeric
1 level tsp chilli powder
4 bay leaves
1 tsp ghee
4 tsps mustard oil preferably
4 cups (1000 ml) water

Soak chick peas **overnight**. Next day wash and drain. Add again fresh water with soda
bicarb. Soak for another hour.

Heat oil and fry potato cubes. Drain and keep aside.

To the same oil add cumin seeds and after a few seconds, add big cardamoms and
sliced coconuts. Fry for a few minutes, add onion and fry until golden in colour. Add
garlic paste and coriander-cumin paste and fry until brown. Add turmeric, fried potato
cubes, yoghurt and sugar stirring frequently. Fry until the oil begins to seperate.

Add chick peas, bay leaves and salt. Mix well. Pour in water. Reduce heat. Cover and
cook until chick peas are tender.

Remove from fire, add garam masala and ghee. Mix well. Serve hot.

ote: If using mustard oil, while heating wait until all foam from the surface disappears.

ooking time: 1½ hours   To serve: 4-6

Sundal

A classic dish of Karnataka prepared for festivals or on 'Holi' in temples.
After being offered to God, this is given as prasad to the devotees.

1½ cups (225 gms) white chick peas (kabuli chana)
½ fresh coconut, grated
½ level tsp ground turmeric
1½ lt water
1¼ level tsps salt
1 tsp coriander leaves, finely chopped

For tadka
3 tsps sesame oil
1 tsp mustard seeds
¼ tsp asafoetida
2 green chillies, seeded and chopped
6 curry leaves

☆ Soak chick peas **overnight**. Drain and place them in a heavy bottom pan with water, turmeric and salt. Bring to a boil, then reduce heat. Cover and boil for 1½ hours, until peas are tender but retain shape.

☆ Remove excess water from cooked peas.

☆ Prepare the tadka just before serving. Heat the oil in a pan to smoking point. Add mustard seeds. After a few seconds add asafoetida, green chillies, and curry leaves, and half the coconut. Stir well and add drained chick peas. Increase heat and fry for few minutes.

☆ Place chick peas in a serving dish and sprinkle remaining coconut and coriander leaves on top.

Cooking time: 2 hours   To serve: 4-6   Picture on page:

Lobia

Black eyed beans with gravy

1½ cups (225 gms) black eyed beans, **soaked overnight**
2 medium onions, chopped, 2 tsps fresh ginger, grated, 3 cloves garlic, crushed and 2 green chillies, seeded and chopped — ground to a paste

1 level tsp ground coriander
½ level tsp ground turmeric
1 level tsp nigella seeds
1½ level tsp salt
3 tbsps plain yoghurt
3 ¾ cups (900 ml) water

1 tsp coriander leaves, finely chopped
4 tsps vegetable oil or melted ghee
4 medium tomatoes, sliced
1 level tsp cumin seeds

☆ Drain the soaked beans.
☆ Heat oil or ghee, add cumin seeds and nigella and after a few seconds, add ground masala. Stirring continuously fry until colour turns golden brown. Sprinkle little water if the mixture begins to stick to the bottom of the pan. Fry until oil separates.
☆ Add coriander, turmeric and salt. Now add 1 tbsp yoghurt at a time. Stir well before adding each spoon yoghurt and fry until oil separates from the mixture.
☆ Add black eyed beans. Mix well and pour water. Cover and simmer over low heat until beans are tender.
☆ Sprinkle coriander leaves before serving. Put tomato slices around. Serve hot.

Cooking time: 1 hour 25 minutes   To serve: 4

Fazita

Marwar

4 mangoes (semi-ripe)	3 level tsps salt
4 cups (1 lt) water	2 level tsps roasted cumin seeds powder
2 tsps chilli powder	Pinch of asafoetida
2 tsps sugar	Oil

- ☆ Cook the mangoes in boiling water until soft.
- ☆ Cut the top, squeeze out all the pulp with seeds.
- ☆ Add 5½ cups of water, mix well.
- ☆ Heat oil in a pan, add asafoetida and chilli powder. Pour in all the mango pulp and water mixture.
- ☆ Add sugar, salt and cumin powder. Cook for 15 minutes and remove from fire. Serve hot

---

Cooking time: 45 minutes   To serve: 5-6   Picture on page: 10

Tadkewali Dal

1 cup red splitted gram dal	1 tsp cumin seeds	A pinch of asafoetida
2 onions, chopped	2 tsps chilli powder	2 tbsps coriander leaves, chopped
6 cloves garlic, finely cut	2 tsps salt	
2 tsps ginger, grated	1 tsp sugar	4 tbsps ghee
4 green chillies, finely cut	10 curry leaves	Water

- ☆ Clean and wash dal, add enough water, half the onions with sugar and salt and cook over slow fire until soft. Mash and mix.
- ☆ Heat ghee in a pan, add asafoetida, cumin seeds, chilli powder, curry leaves, onion, ginger, garlic. Fry until brown.
- ☆ Now pour the mixture over the dal.
- ☆ Garnish with coriander and green chillies.

Cooking time: 25 minutes   To serve: 4-6   Picture on page: 12

Tez Sabzi Kari

Hot vegetable curry

small cauliflower, separate the
owerettes
medium size potatoes, peeled and
ut into big cubes
2 cup peas
00 gms french beans, cut into 1"
eces
medium onion, chopped

6 cloves garlic, crushed
6 green chillies, chopped
3 red chillies, 1 tsp cumin seeds,
8 peppercorns, 4 cloves, 1" piece
cinnamon, 2 green cardamoms and
1 tsp coriander seeds — dry roasted
and ground to a smooth paste

2 bay leaves
½ cup ghee
2 tbsps coriander leaves,
chopped

Heat ghee and fry cauliflower, beans and potatoes until light brown. Remove from fire
and keep aside.

Fry onion, garlic, chillies and bay leaves separately. Add beans, cauliflower, potatoes
and peas. Mix well.

Add all ground spices, stir well and fry for 10-15 minutes.

Add 2 cups hot water, cover and simmer over low flame for another 10 minutes until
gravy is thick.

Remove from fire and sprinkle chopped coriander.

Cooking time: 25 minutes   To serve: 4-6

Mewa Rasedar

Exotic dry fruits in a spicy gravy

12 dried apricots, soaked in water for
10 minutes
12 dried figs, soaked in water for
5 minutes
12 prunes
50 gms cashewnuts
50 gms almonds
3 medium onions, chopped

50 gms raisins or sultanas
15 crystallised red cherries
2 large tomatoes, halved
6 cloves garlic and 1" piece ginger,
ground together
2 tbsps Kashmiri chilli powder
1 tsp cumin seeds
1 tsp turmeric powder

25 gms broken cashewnuts
and 25 gms poppy seeds,
ground to a paste
4 tbsps single cream
275 gms butter
1 level tsp salt
2 cups (425 ml) water

☆ Melt butter, fry onions until lightly browned. Add poppy seeds and cashewnut paste, garlic and ginger paste and saute for 3 minutes.

☆ Add tomatoes, stir well and fry for 10 minutes.

☆ Add cumin seeds, turmeric, salt, chilli and water. Cook over low heat until gravy becomes a little thick.

☆ Add figs, apricots, prunes, cashewnuts, almonds, cherries and raisins. Cook for five minutes. Remove from heat.

☆ Before serving add cream. Serve hot with mughlai paratha.

Cooking time: 25 minutes   To serve: 4-6   Picture on page: 2(

138

Kashmiri Methi Chaman

Cottage cheese and fenugreek leaves cooked with oriental spices

50 gms fenugreek leaves (methi)
50 gms fresh spinach, discard the hard stems
300 gms cottage cheese (see page 17)
A pinch of asafoetida

5 cloves
1 level tsp cumin seeds
½ level tsp ground turmeric
1 level tbsp fresh ginger, grated
½ level tsp dry ginger (soonth)
1 level tsp Kashmiri chilli powder

1 green chilli, seeded and chopped
1 level tsp ground coriander
½ tsp garam masala (see page 19)
1½ level tsps salt
2 cups (425 ml) water
Ghee or oil

* Clean, wash and roughly chop spinach and fenugreek leaves. Grind to a smooth paste.
* Cut the cottage cheese into fingers like potato finger chips.
* Heat ghee or oil, fry cheese fingers until pale golden brown. Drain and keep aside.
* Heat 4 tbsps oil, add asafoetida, cumin and cloves. After few seconds, add ground spinach and fenugreek paste. Fry over medium heat, stirring continuously until cooked.
* Add turmeric, chilli, ginger, dry ginger, salt, ground coriander and water.
* Simmer for few minutes. As the gravy begins to thicken, add fried cheese fingers. Reduce heat and simmer over low heat until the gravy is thick.
* Transfer to serving dish, sprinkle coriander leaves. Serve hot.

Cooking time: 30 minutes   To serve: 4-6   Picture on page: 120

Paneer Sultani

300 gms paneer
450 gms tomatoes, blanched, seeded and chopped
1 medium onion, finely chopped
½ tsp turmeric powder

½ tsp chilli powder
3 cloves
3 cardamoms, crushed
1 level tsp salt
1 tbsp sugar
½ tsp black cumin seeds
1 tsp garlic, chopped

5 tbsps hot water
4 tbsps oil
1 tbsp coriander leaves, chopped

* Cut the paneer into slices ½" (1 cm) thick and 2" × 2" in size.
* Heat oil in a pan add black cumin seeds, garlic, onion, chilli and turmeric powder, cloves, cardamoms and tomatoes. Cover and simmer over low heat. Make a thick gravy, add salt and sugar.
* Add cut paneer slices. Simmer for 5 minutes and remove from heat. Garnish with chopped coriander.

Cooking time: 30 minutes   To serve: 4-6

Baingan Kalwa

Sweet and spicy brinjal speciality of Gujarat

450 gms brinjals
1 cup (100 gms) gram flour
1 tbsp sugar

2 red Kashmiri chillies, dry roasted and powdered
1 level tsp turmeric powder
1" piece of ginger

A pinch of asafoetida
5 tbsps (75 gms) broken cashewnuts
7 tbsps oil

* Wash and cut brinjals (do not remove skin) into cubes.
* Heat oil in a pan. Fry cut brinjals until tender, remove and place on a kitchen paper.
* Remove half the oil from pan and add all other ingredients except brinjals. Saute for 4-5 minutes.
* Add brinjals and cook for 5 minutes. Serve hot.

Cooking time: 20 minutes   To serve: 4-6

Mughlai Phulgobi

Cauliflower stuffed with solidified milk, nuts and spices

medium cauliflower
5 medium ripe tomatoes, blanched, chopped and pureed
3 medium onions, grated
1 cup (100 gms) khoya (see page 17)
7 tbsps plain yoghurt
10 cloves garlic and 2 level tbsps poppy seeds, dry roasted and ground together

2 tbsps fresh ginger, grated, with 2 green chillies, seeded and chopped — ground to a smooth paste
25 gms almonds, blanched and fried
Pinch of nutmeg
½ tsp turmeric powder
½ tsp nigella seeds (kalonji)
1½ level tsps salt
½ level tsp chilli powder

2 tbsps raisins, soaked and drained
6 strands of saffron soaked in 1 tbsp milk
2 tbsps fresh coriander leaves, chopped
Ghee or oil
1 tbsp salt for gravy
Cream

* Break off the stalks of the cauliflower from central core.
* Pour enough water to cover the cauliflower in a large pan and mix salt. Soak the cauliflower in it for 30 minutes.
* Heat ghee or oil. Put nigella seeds and as they pop and splutter, add onion and fry until light brown.
* Add ground ginger-chilli mixture, stir well and fry for few minutes. Add ground garlic mixture and khoya and fry until colour turns golden brown.
* Add yoghurt. Stirring frequently, fry again until oil begins to separate. Add chilli, salt and raisins.
* Pour in the tomato puree, mix well. Simmer until done. Add saffron solution and nutmeg. Cool slightly.
* Stuff the masala in between the flowerettes very carefully without breaking the cauliflower.
* Keep remaining masala aside.
* Heat 8 tbsps oil, place the stuffed cauliflower upside down, sprinkle little water, reduce heat. Cover and cook for 10 minutes.
* Turn and cook until tender. Do not overcook or it will break.
* Place remaining masala in a deep serving dish, put the cauliflower in the centre. Apply the cream on top and sprinkle fried almonds, coriander leaves. Serve hot.

Cooking time: 35 minutes   To serve: 4-6

Punjabi Khumbi Alu

Fresh mushrooms with new potatoes cooked in Punjabi style

450 gms fresh small white mushrooms
450 gms small new potatoes
2 medium onions, sliced
3 cloves garlic, crushed and 1 tsp fresh ginger, grated — ground to a paste
1 level tsp ground turmeric

1 level tsp garam masala (see page 19)
1 level tsp cumin seeds
½ level tsp chilli powder
1 level tsp coriander powder
1 level tsp cumin seeds, roasted and ground

1½ level tsps salt
3 large cardamoms pods
2 tsps fresh coriander or parsley leaves, finely chopped
2 tomatoes, chopped
4 tsps melted ghee or oil
Hot water

* Clean mushrooms. Wash thoroughly. Cut the woody part of the stem. If the mushrooms are large, cut into halves or quarters leaving a piece of stalk on each mushroom.
* Soak potatoes in water for few minutes. Wash and scrub them well. Cut the large potatoes into half.
* Heat ghee or oil in a pan. Fry onion, cumin seeds and cardamoms until brown. Add garlic-ginger paste and fry for a few minutes. Add tomatoes, ground cumin, coriander, stir and fry until the paste become brown and thick and the oil separates from it.
* Add turmeric, chilli and salt, stir well.
* Add potatoes and mushrooms, fry for few minutes.
* Add water, cover and simmer over low heat for 10 minutes.
* Remove cover, and increase heat. Stir well. Cook until potatoes are tender and the gravy becomes thick. Sprinkle garam masala.
* Serve hot, garnished with chopped coriander.

Cooking time: 30 minutes   To serve: 4-6

Hyderabadi Bagharu Baingan

A classic Mughlai dish of Hyderabad

-8 small round brinjals
medium onions
tsps ginger, grated
cloves garlic, chopped
tsp grated coconut or desiccated
2 level tsp fenugreek seeds (methi
ana)

1 level tsp ground coriander
1 tsp shelled peanuts
1 level tsp cumin seeds
1 level tsp sesame seeds
1 level tsp poppy seeds
½ tsp ground turmeric
6 curry leaves

1 level tsp chilli powder
1 level tsp salt
4 tsps tamarind pulp (see page 20)
8 tsps vegetable oil
1 tsp coriander leaves, finely chopped

Wash and pat dry the brinjals. Carefully slit them into four lengthways — do not cut right through, they should be held together at the stalk.

Heat oil in a frying pan. Fry the brinjals for a few minutes until light brown, turn once. Remove from oil and place them on a kitchen paper.

Thread onions in a skewer and grill over glowing coal or place skewer under a grill. Peel the charred skin and chop.

Grind together onion, garlic, ginger, poppy seeds, peanuts, sesame seeds, half of the cumin seeds, coriander and coconut. Make a fine paste.

Heat remaining oil again. Put remaining cumin seeds and fenugreek seeds and curry leaves. Then add ground onion paste. Stir well. Fry for few minutes.

Add salt, turmeric and chilli. Cook over medium heat until oil begins to separate and colour turns brown.

Stir in tamarind juice. Mix well and cook for another few minutes.

Gently add fried brinjals, coat evenly with the masala mixture. Cover and reduce heat. Cook another 10 minutes.

Serve hot. Garnish with chopped coriander leaves.

---

ooking time: 35 minutes   To serve: 4-6

Shahi Navratan Korma

Seasonal vegetable curry with cottage cheese

225 gms cottage cheese (paneer), cubed
225 gms yellow pumpkin, peeled and diced
100 gms shelled peas
175 gms yam, peeled and diced
4 medium potatoes, peeled and diced
50 gms puffed lotus seeds (makhanas)

100 gms carrots, diced
4 large onions, sliced
2 tsps raisins
2 green chillies, seeded and chopped
8 cloves garlic, 1″ piece ginger and 1 tsp cumin seeds, ground to a paste
1 cup (250 ml) plain yoghurt
1 tsp garam masala (see page 19)

4 cloves
1″ piece cinnamon
1 tsp sugar
½ tsp turmeric powder
Juice of two lemons
6 tsps oil
1½ tsps salt
2 tbsps coriander leaves, finely chopped

* Heat oil in a pan, add sugar, allow it to brown, add yam, peas, pumpkin, potato and carrots. Stir well and fry until colour of vegetables turns brown. Remove from oil. Place them on a kitchen paper.
* In same oil fry cottage cheese pieces until brown and remove from oil.
* Fry onions until brown, add cloves and cinnamon. After a few seconds add ground paste and fry until the mixture turns brown. Stir in salt, turmeric, garam masala and green chillies. Mix well.
* Add vegetables, raisins, lotus seeds with ½ cup (125 ml) water. Cover and cook over low heat for 15 minutes.
* Beat curd lightly and pour it on the vegetables. Mix well. Cook for a few minutes. The gravy should be thick. Keep stirring.
* Add lemon juice. Serve hot. Garnish with chopped coriander leaves.

Cooking time: 45 minutes   To serve: 4-6

Mughlai Kofta Rasedar

Royal dish of cottage cheese balls stuffed with nuts and cooked in a spicy sauce

2 cups (225 gms) cottage cheese
2 level tbsps gram flour
2 tbsps raisins, wash and drain well
8 almonds, blanched and chopped
½ level tsp chilli powder
1 level tsp salt
2 tbsps plain flour
Ghee or oil

For gravy
1 level tbsp poppy seeds, 8 cloves garlic, 2 tbsps fresh ginger, grated and ground to a paste
6 tomatoes, blanched and chopped
½ level tsp onion seeds (kalonji)
6 whole cloves
2 sticks of cinnamon
4 small green cardamoms, shelled and crushed
2 large onions, grated
1 level tsp coriander seeds, ground
1 level tsp cumin seeds, ground

½ cup cream
2 level tsps chilli powder
1 level tsp turmeric powder
1½ level tsps salt
25 gms almonds, blanched and slivered
2 cups water
½ tsp garam masala (see page 19)
2 tbsps fresh coriander, finely chopped
Ghee or oil

- Crumble the cottage cheese and knead until smooth. Mix gram flour, chilli and salt.
- Shape them into balls. Make a depression in the middle. Press one or two raisins (raisins should be dry) and few pieces of almonds in the depression. Carefully shape them into round balls again. Coat them with flour.
- Heat oil. Deep fry the cottage cheese balls until all sides turn brown. Drain and keep on a kitchen paper.
- Heat 6 tbsps oil, put the cardamoms, cloves, kalonji and cinnamon into the hot oil. Within seconds the cloves will expand.
- Add onions. Stir and fry the onions until brown. Reduce heat and stir in ginger and poppy seeds paste. Fry until golden brown. Add 1 tbsp water.
- Add ground coriander, cumin, chilli, salt, turmeric and after few seconds put in the tomatoes. Stir constantly and fry till oil separates. Pour in the cream gently, stirring constantly.
- Add water and bring to a boil. Cover and simmer over low heat for 10 minutes and remove.
- Fifteen minutes before serving, heat the gravy, add fried cheese koftas. Transfer to a deep serving dish.
- Sprinkle almonds and coriander leaves on top. Makhanas (lotus seeds) can be added for special occasions.

Cooking time: 30-35 minutes   To serve: 4-6

Ghassey

Dry potato fingers with garlic

450 gms potatoes
8 garlic cloves, lightly crushed
4 tbsps melted ghee or oil
1 tbsp split black gram (urad dal)

6 curry leaves
3 Kashmiri red chillies
1 level tsp salt

* Scrub and wash potatoes, cut them into very thin 1" (2.5 cms) long finger chips. Wash thoroughly and drain well.
* Heat oil or ghee in a pan and fry garlic over low heat until light brown. Add urad dal, curry leaves and chillies and fry for a few seconds.
* Add potatoes and salt. Mix well. Cover and fry over low heat, until chips are tender, stirring occasionally. If necessary sprinkle little water during cooking.

| Cooking time: 18 minutes | To serve: 4-6 | Picture on page: 101 |

Mangalorean Tambli Bhaji

Red spinach cooked with coconut spices in Mangalorean style

225 gms red spinach
½ fresh coconut, grated and ground
3 green chillies, seeded and chopped
Pinch of asafoetida

½ tsp cumin seeds
6 tbsps tamarind pulp
1 tsp salt
1 tbsp oil
1¼ cups (275 ml) water

* Clean and discard fibrous stem of spinach. Wash thoroughly. Cut the stalks into ½" length.
* Place spinach and chillies in a pan cover and cook over medium heat. Add water only if required. Remove from fire when done.
* Mix tamarind, ground coconut and spinach and grind into a smooth paste.
* Heat oil, fry cumin seeds and asafoetida. Stir in spinach paste with water. Boil slowly over medium heat for few minutes. Remove from fire and serve hot.

| Cooking time: 30 minutes | To serve: 4-6 |

Tamatar Hyderabadi

Stuffed tomatoes Hyderabadi style

firm ripe large tomatoes
tbsp lime juice
tbsps mashed cottage cheese
(paneer)
tbsps cashewnuts, crushed lightly
tbsps raisins
tbsps tomato puree or sauce

1 onion, sliced
½ tsp salt
4 cloves, crushed
1 piece cinnamon
1 green chilli, seeded and chopped
¼ tsp ground black pepper

2 tbsps ghee or oil
6 tbsps cream optional
4 tbsps coconut, freshly grated
2 tbsps coriander, finely
chopped

Wash the tomatoes and wipe them dry. Slice the top carefully. Scoop out inside pulp.
Sprinkle lemon juice and dash of salt inside each tomato.
Heat ghee or oil in a pan. Fry onion until brown. Add cinnamon, cloves, raisins,
cashewnuts, pepper and green chilli. Stir well and fry for few minutes.
Stir in the cottage cheese (paneer) and tomato puree or sauce. Mix well stirring
constantly and fry for 5 minutes more.
Stuff the tomatoes with the cheese mixture and cover the tops with cream.
Bake in a pre-heated oven (375° F-190° C-Gas Mark 4) for 10 minutes.
Serve hot or cold. Garnish with grated coconut and coriander.

Cooking time: 20 minutes   To serve: 4-6

Punjabi Palak ke Kofte

Spinach balls in a spicy gravy cooked Punjabi style

For koftas
175 gms fresh spinach leaves
225 gms gram flour (besan)
1 tsp cumin seeds and 1 tsp
coriander seeds, ground to a paste
½ tsp salt
½ tsp chilli powder
1 tbsp poppy seeds and 2 tbsps
broken cashewnuts, ground together
⅝ cup (150 ml) water
Oil for deep frying

For gravy
3 ripe tomatoes
1 tsp chilli powder
1 medium onion, chopped
6 cloves garlic, crushed
1 tbsp ginger, finely chopped
1 tsp cumin seeds
½ tsp turmeric powder

1 level tsp salt
1 tbsp coriander leaves, finely
chopped
3 tbsps vegetable oil
2½ cups (575 ml) water
1 tbsp single cream
2 tbsps broken cashewnuts,
fried

To make gravy

☆ Heat oil in a pan, add cumin seeds and as they splutter add onion, garlic, ginger. Stir all the time. Fry until colour turns brown. Add turmeric, salt, chilli and after one minute add tomatoes. Keep stirring and fry until tomatoes are reduced to a pulp. If mixture sticks to the bottom of the pan add 1 or 2 spoons of water.

☆ Pour in remaining water, bring it to a boil, then reduce the heat, allow it to simmer gently uncovered for 10 minutes.

To make koftas

☆ Wash the spinach leaves. Discard yellow leaves, if any. Pat them dry with a kitchen towel.

☆ Chop the spinach very finely or grind roughly.

☆ Mix gram flour, spinach, chilli, poppy seeds and cashewnut paste, cumin and coriander paste, and salt together in a bowl. Add water a little at a time. Make a fairly stiff dough.

☆ Take 2 tsps of spinach mixture and shape into a small ball. Repeat the same with remaining dough.

☆ Heat oil in a pan. Fry spinach koftas over low heat, few at a time, until golden brown in colour. Remove them to a kitchen paper.

☆ Add fried koftas to the sauce. Cover and simmer again for 15 minutes over low heat.

☆ Place them on a deep serving plate and add cream on top just before serving. Garnish with coriander leaves and cashewnuts.

Cooking time: 45 minutes   To serve: 4-6

Bhutte ki Sabzi

Corn curry

50 gms tender corn kernels, boiled
½ fresh coconut, grated or 75 gms
esiccated coconut
tbsps poppy seeds

1 tbsp peanuts
1 tsp cumin seeds
1 tsp coriander seeds
2 green chillies

1 inch piece of ginger
3 tbsps oil
2 level tsps salt
4 cups (1 lt) coconut milk (see page 17)
2 medium tomatoes, sliced for garnishing

Extract coconut milk from 5 fresh coconuts.
Grind together poppy seeds, cumin seeds, peanuts, coriander seeds, chillies, ginger and fresh coconut. Make a fine paste.
Heat oil, fry the ground paste until golden colour.
Add boiled corn kernels and coconut milk. Cook over low fire for 10 minutes till gravy becomes quite thick. Add salt.
Serve hot, garnished with tomato slices.

ooking time: 30 minutes	To serve: 4-6	Picture on page: 34

Ambal

Sweet and sour tomatoes of Bengal

2 kg tomatoes, chopped
tbsps sugar
level tsp of panch phoran (see
age 18)
tbsp raisins

1 level tsp salt
Pinch of turmeric powder
2 bay leaves
Water
2 tbsps ghee or oil

Heat ghee in a heavy pan. Add bay leaves, panch phoran and tomatoes. Fry few minutes.
Add salt, raisins, turmeric and sugar. Stir well and cook for 5 minutes.
Add 1 cup water, cover and simmer over medium heat for 10 minutes. Remove from heat and serve hot.

ooking time: 20 minutes	To serve: 4

149

Aviyal

A Malabari preparation of mixed vegetables with yoghurt

450 gms mixed vegetables, cut into julienne strips (carrots, fresh beans, capsicums, brinjal, cucumber, pumpkins, zucchini, unripe banana, yam, drumsticks, etc.)
1 green mango, peeled and sliced (optional)

1 cup (100 gms) grated fresh coconut or desiccated
1 level tsp cumin seeds
5 green chillies, cut lengthways (optional)
1 tsp garlic, chopped

1½ tsps salt
5 tbsps coconut oil
1 cup (250 ml) yoghurt
1 sprig curry leaves
½ tsp turmeric powder
2½ cups (575 ml) water

* Bring the water to a boil, add cut vegetables, turmeric and mango slices. Simmer over low heat until vegetables are tender. Remove vegetables from water. Keep the liquid.
* Grind together coconut, cumin seeds, garlic, chillies to a paste.
* Heat the remaining vegetables stock and add ground paste, salt, curry leaves and bring to a boil.
* Add boiled vegetables gently and stir well. Add yoghurt. Cook 2 minutes more, then remove from fire.
* Add hot coconut oil and mix gently.

Note: Aviyal is prepared for mass feedings (langar) in large brass vessels of 10 ft diameter and 5ft depth in South Indian temples of Sri Padmanabha Swami.

Cooking time: 25 minutes   To serve: 4-6

Vegetable Khatkhate

Karwari Saraswat style

50 gms horse radish, diced
50 gms sweet potatoes, diced
50 gms yellow pumpkin, diced
50 gms cucumber, diced
50 gms french beans, cut into
1" pieces
50 gms spinach (only tender stalks)
2 drumsticks, cut into 1" pieces

25 gms black eyed beans (chowli)
50 gms snake gourd, diced
3 green chillies, seeded and slit
4 pieces kokum (see page 24)
2 tbsps jaggery
1 tbsp coconut oil
2 level tsps salt
7 teflan (see page 24)

Ground to a paste
4 Kashmiri or Goa chillies
½ fresh coconut, grated
¼ tsp turmeric powder

- Clean and soak chowli beans **overnight**.
  Boil with enough water until tender.
- Add above vegetables one by one. If necessary add little more water. Stir well. Simmer over low heat until vegetables are half done.
- Add ground paste, salt, jaggery, kokum and teflan. Simmer again over low heat until done.
- Add green chillies. Stir well. Remove from heat add coconut oil (unheated). Mix thoroughly. Serve hot.

Cooking time: 1 hour | To serve: 4-6

151

Karwari Simla Mirch Panchamrit

Capsicums with roasted coconut, peanuts and oriental spices in Karwari Saraswat style

8 medium capsicums
4 tbsps shelled peanuts, dry roasted
and skin removed
1 tbsp jaggery
A pinch of asafoetida
½ tsp black mustard seeds
10 curry leaves
4 tbsps oil
1 tsp salt

Ground to a fine paste
½ fresh coconut, grated and dry
roasted
1 tbsp split bengal gram
2 tsps split black gram
1 tbsp sesame seeds
¼ tsp turmeric powder
1 tsp coriander seeds
3 tbsps tamarind pulp (see page
20)
6-8 tbsps water

* ☆ Cut the capsicums into strips lengthways.
* ☆ Heat oil in a pan, add mustard seeds, asafoetida and curry leaves.
* ☆ As mustard seeds splutter, add cut capsicums and fry for 5 minutes. Stir in all ground ingredients, peanuts, jaggery and salt. Simmer over low heat for 15 minutes, till gravy is thick. Serve hot.

Cooking time: 20 minutes   To serve: 4-6

Facing Page
Clockwise:

Baroda Dal Dhok
Aluwala Roti

Sindhi Sai Bhaji

A highly nutritious mixed vegetable dish

0 gms spinach
0 gms fenugreek leaves
5 gms dill leaves (sua bhaji)
medium tomatoes, chopped
medium potatoes, peeled and
iced
medium onion, chopped

1 tbsp fresh ginger, grated
6 cloves garlic, chopped
3 tbsps split chick peas (chana dal),
soaked
4 tbsps shelled peas ⎱ Optional
1 medium carrot ⎰
1 level tsp salt

½ level tsp turmeric
1 level tsp dhania-zeera (see
page 19)
2 tbsps fresh coriander leaves,
finely chopped
3 tbsps oil or ghee
5/8 cup (150 ml) water

- Wash and drain soaked dal.
- Clean and wash spinach, fenugreek and dill. Discard any hard stems and chop finely.
- Place together spinach, fenugreek, dill, tomatoes, potatoes, carrot, peas, onion, salt and turmeric in a pressure cooker with water. Put on the lid and bring steadily to one pressure. Reduce heat and cook 15 minutes.
- Allow pressure to return to normal before removing the lid. Open the lid and mix the mixture thoroughly.
- Heat oil, fry garlic and ginger. Sprinkle dhania-zeera and pour it over the vegetable mixture. Simmer for 10 minutes.
- Serve hot, garnished with coriander.

---

ooking time: 35 minutes   To serve: 4-6   Picture on page: 33

Lucknowi Dahi Bade

Stuffed tender dumplings in spicy yoghurt sauce

¾ cup (175 gms) split black gram, without skin
½ cup (100 gms) split green gram, without skin
1½ lt lukewarm water and 1 tsp salt, mixed together
1 tsp chilli powder
½ tsp ground coriander
½ tsp cumin seeds, roasted and ground
1½ level tsps salt
1 recipe imly chutney mathurawale (see page 232)

Oil for deep frying

For stuffing
25 gms raisins, soaked and chopped
3 tbsps coriander leaves, finely chopped
1 medium onion, grated
4 tbsps fresh ginger, finely grated
3 green chillies, seeded and chopped

For garnishing
2 tbsps fresh coriander leaves, finely chopped

For yoghurt mix
2 cups (500 ml) plain yoghurt
⅝ cup (150 ml) water
1 level tsp cumin seeds, roasted and ground
1 level tsp salt
1½ level tsps sugar

* Soak dals **overnight**. Wash next day thoroughly. Place dals in a blender and grind to a paste, adding a little water at a time to ease the grinding.
* Drop 1 tsp of the paste into a bowl of cold water to test if the paste is of the right consistency. It should rise to the surface.
* Add salt and chilli powder to the dal paste and beat well.
* Make imly chutney and chill.
* Beat yoghurt, water, cumin, sugar and salt. Chill slightly.
* Heat oil in deep frying pan.
* Place a piece of wet cotton cloth on a hard surface. Keep a bowl of cold water nearby.
* Place a tablespoon of the dal paste on the wet cloth. Wet your fingers and pat it to a round shape. Place 1 tsp of the stuffing in the centre. Now tilt the cloth and fold the paste in half over it. Cover the stuffing completely.
* Again wet your fingers and place over the bada and carefully prise away the stuffed bada. Repeat with the remaining paste one by one.
* Carefully lower the badas, a few at a time, into the hot oil. Fry to a golden colour turning once or twice. Remove from oil and keep on a kitchen paper for one minute then put into the salted water. When the badas sink and remain at the bottom, take them out one by one and press gently between your palms to squeeze out the water.
* Dip them in the yoghurt mix for 5 minutes and place them in a deep serving dish. Keep in a cool place.
* Ten minutes before serving, spoon the remaining yoghurt sauce over the badas and then gently spoon the imly chutney over it.
* Sprinkle chilli powder, roasted and ground cumin powder, and coriander leaves.

Cooking time: 30 minutes   Makes: 20

Kaju ki Kari

Spicy raw cashewnut curry of South India

225 gms green cashewnuts
1" piece fresh ginger, 1 tsp poppy
seeds, 2 medium onions, 2 green
chillies, seeded and 4 cloves garlic
— ground to a paste

1 level tsp salt
3 tomatoes, chopped
6 tbsps oil
2 cups (425 ml) coconut milk

2 tsps fresh mint or coriander,
finely chopped

* Peel cashewnuts carefully, try to keep them whole.
* Heat 4 tbsps oil. Fry the nuts until light golden in colour. Remove and keep them aside.
* Heat remaining oil, fry the ground masala until golden brown. Add salt and tomatoes. Stir well. Fry until oil begins to separate.
* Add cashewnuts and coconut milk. Cook over medium heat until the gravy is thick.
* Serve hot, garnished with coriander.

Cooking time: 25 minutes   To serve: 4-6   Picture on page: 119

Gucchi Badshahi

Black mushrooms, potatoes and green peas curry

225 gms dry Kashmiri mushrooms, **soaked overnight**
6 medium potatoes, peeled and halved
2 large ripe tomatoes
¼ cup (50 gms) shelled peas (optional)
2 medium onions, finely chopped
2 tsps cumin seeds, 2 tbsps fresh ginger grated and 1 green chilli — ground to a paste

1 level tsp turmeric
1 level tsp chilli powder
1½ level tsps salt
4 cloves garlic and 1 tbsp poppy seeds, ground to a fine paste

2 (1″ long) pieces cinnamon
3 cloves, crushed
3 cardamoms, shelled and crushed
2 bay leaves
4 tbsps oil
3 cups (750 ml) water
2 tbsps fresh mint leaves, shredded

☆ Wash and drain mushrooms. Discard the woody stalks.

☆ Heat oil, fry onions for a few minutes, add cinnamon, cloves and cardamoms. Stir in ground cumin-ginger paste and fry until light brown. Add ground poppy seeds-garlic paste. Stir frequently and fry until deep brown.

☆ Add tomatoes and fry again over medium heat until the oil begins to separate. Add chilli powder, turmeric and bay leaves. Stir well.

☆ Add potatoes stirring continuously and fry for few minutes. Add mushrooms and peas with water. Cover and simmer until tender.

☆ Serve hot garnished with shredded fresh mint leaves.

Cooking time: 35 minutes   To serve: 4-6

Shahi Mattar Paneer

Royal dish of peas and cottage cheese

2 cups (250 gms) cottage cheese, cut into small cubes
1 cup (115 gms) khoya, mashed (see page 17)
2 cups (250 gms) shelled peas
25 gms makhanas (puffed lotus seeds)
A pinch of asafoetida

10 cloves garlic
1 level tsp cumin seeds
1 level tsp ground coriander
1 level tsp chili powder
1 level tsp dry ginger powder
1 level tsp garam masala (see page 19)
1 tbsp fresh ginger, grated

1 green chilli, seeded and chopped
3 tbsps fresh coriander leaves, finely chopped
1½ level tsps salt
Oil for frying
2½ cups (575 ml) water

* Heat 5 tbsps of oil, fry the cottage cheese cubes lightly. Drain and keep aside.
* Add little more oil and fry the makhanas. Drain and keep aside.
* Add asafoetida, cumin seeds, garlic and khoya to the hot oil. Fry over low heat until colour turns reddish brown.
* Add coriander, green and red chilli, grated and dry ginger, garam masala and salt. Stir well for few seconds and add peas, and makhanas with water. Cover and simmer for 15 minutes.
* Put in the fried cheese cubes. Simmer again for 20 minutes.
* Sprinkle chopped coriander leaves and cook for 5 minutes more.
* Serve hot.

Cooking time: 45 minutes   To serve: 4-6

Kofta Alu Bukhara

Potato and cottage cheese balls stuffed with
dried prunes cooked in spicy sauce

For koftas
4 medium potatoes, boiled, peeled and mashed
1 cup (115 gms) mashed cottage cheese
1 tbsp flour
1 tbsp cumin seeds, roasted and ground
1 level tsp salt
10-12 dried prunes, **soaked overnight and stoned**
Oil for deep frying

For gravy
2 large tomatoes, chopped
2 medium onions, grated
8 cloves garlic, crushed
1 tbsp ginger, grated
1 tsp chilli powder
1 level tsp salt
½ tsp ground black pepper
½ tsp turmeric powder

2 heaped tbsps poppy seeds and 2 tbsps broken cashewnuts, ground to a paste
2 tbsps single cream
3 tbsps oil
2 tbsps coriander leaves, finely chopped

★ Mix together mashed potatoes, mashed cottage cheese, ground cumin, salt and flour. Knead well and make a smooth dough.

★ Divide the dough into 10-12 parts, shape them into round balls.

★ Wash the soaked prunes and wipe them well.

★ Make a depression in the centre of each ball and place a prune on each. Now carefully close and shape into round balls.

★ Heat oil and fry cheese balls until colour turns golden brown. Drain and keep them on a kitchen paper.

★ Heat 3 tbsps oil and fry onions until transparent. Add garlic and ginger, stir well and fry till colour turns light brown. Add tomato and stir for 2 minutes. Add chilli, black pepper, turmeric, stir for a minute. Add poppy seed mixture stirring well and fry till oil begins to separate.

★ Pour in water. Cover and simmer over low heat for 15 minutes.

★ Add fried cheese balls. Remove cover. Simmer over low heat for another 15 minutes to thicken the gravy.

★ Spoon the cream just before serving and sprinkle coriander leaves.

Cooking time: 1 hour   To serve: 4-6

Khatta Kaddo

Sweet and sour yellow pumpkin

450 gms yellow pumpkin, peeled and seeded
2 large ripe tomatoes, chopped
2 medium onions, finely chopped
1 level tsp cumin seeds

1 tbsp fresh ginger, finely grated
½ tsp chilli powder
½ tsp turmeric powder
2 level tsps dried mango powder

½ tsp garam masala (see page 19)
1 level tsp salt
2 tbsps vegetable oil
1 green chilli, seeded (optional)

- Cut pumpkin into small squares of 1″ and ½″ thick.
- Heat oil in a pan over high heat. Add cumin seeds and after one minute, add onion and ginger. Reduce the heat and stir constantly till the colour turns golden.
- Add chilli powder, turmeric and salt. Stir well and fry another minute.
- Add tomatoes and fry until soft. Add pumpkin pieces. Mix well. Cover and cook over medium heat and allow to cook in its own juices until pumpkin is soft and tender. Mash a few pieces with a fork and keep few pieces whole.
- Sprinkle mango powder, garam masala and chopped green chilli.

Cooking time: 25 minutes   To serve: 4-6

Mee Ho Lee Khar

Assamese mixed vegetable 'khar'

¼ cup (50 gms) split green gram
100 gms spinach, wash and discard
the hard stalks
½ tsp ground turmeric
1 large carrot, scraped and diced

½ tsp soda bicarb
1 level tsp salt
2 green chillies, seeded and cut
lengthways

1 tsp cumin seeds
2 bay leaves
2 tbsps oil
Water

* Wash and soak moong dal for 10 minutes, drain well and keep aside.
* Heat oil, put in cumin, bay leaves and chillies and as they pop and splutter, add moong dal. Stir and fry for few minutes, add turmeric. Mix well.
* Add spinach and carrot. Add soda bicarb and salt, stir well. Stir and fry for few minutes. Reduce heat, pour in 1½ cups of water. Cover and simmer for 10 minutes. Do not allow spinach to discolour.
* Cook until the dal is tender. Serve hot.

Note: Traditionally 'khar' is cooked with one vegetable and a lot of small fish (not larger than a finger). Khar can also be made with single vegetable — like raw papaya, marrow (lauki), beans, raw banana. This recipe is an all time favourite of the North-Easterns. Traditionally soda bicarb is not used but a solution made from burnt banana ash called kha-ro-ni is used.

Cooking time: 20 minutes   To serve: 4-6

Zaminkand Rasedar

Spicy yam curry

275 gms yam, peeled and cut into
2″ × 2″ cubes
A pinch of asafoetida
6 cloves garlic, crushed
½ level tsp cumin seeds
1 green chilli, seeded and chopped

2 tbsps fresh ginger, grated
½ level tsp dry ginger
1 tsp garam masala
1 tsp ground coriander
1 level tsp salt
1 level tsp chilli powder

½ level tsp turmeric
5½ cups (1.25 lt) water
2 tbsps fresh coriander leaves,
finely chopped
Oil

⋆ Rub little oil on your fingers before cutting yam to prevent itching. Place them in a pan with half the water over medium heat. Cook until tender. Drain and keep aside.

⋆ Heat oil, fry cooked yam pieces until golden brown. Drain and keep them on a kitchen paper.

⋆ Heat 4 tbsps oil. Put asafoetida, cumin and garlic and as they pop and splutter add dry and grated gingers, chillies, ground coriander and turmeric with one cup of water. Bring to boil. Add garam masala.

⋆ Add fried yam pieces with remaining water. Reduce heat. Cover and allow to simmer for 20 minutes until the water evaporates and thick gravy remains.

⋆ Transfer into a serving dish and garnish with chopped coriander.

Cooking time: 35 minutes   To serve: 4-6

Bhareli Simla Mirch

Capsicums stuffed with cheese, chutney, spices and dry fruits

6 medium capsicums
2 tbsps oil

For stuffing
2 cups (220 gms) cottage cheese,
mashed

6 tbsps tomato sauce
4 tbsps mint chutney
6 green chillies, seeded and
chopped
1 level tsp salt

1 tbsp finely sliced garlic (or
dry garlic flakes)
2 tbsps raisins
2 tbsps casheawnuts, broken
Oil

* Mash cottage cheese well, add rest of the ingredients and mix thoroughly.
* Wash and wipe capsicums and rub oil on them. With a very sharp knife, gently make a slit (lengthways) on each capsicum. Scoop out the seeds carefully.
* Stuff the cheese mixture into the capsicums and tie them carefuly with a string.
* Heat oil in a fry pan. Fry stuffed capsicums on all sides. Remove threads and serve hot.

Cooking time: 20 minutes   To serve: 4-6

Kathal ki Kofta Kari

Jackfruit kofta curry

1 kg jackfruit, peeled, boiled and ground
3 tbsps gram flour
Pinch of soda bicarb
2 tsps salt
6 cloves garlic, 4 green chillies, ½ fresh coconut, 1 tsp garam masala — ground together
2 tbsps chopped coriander, for garnishing

For gravy
3 medium onions, chopped
4 cloves garlic, crushed
2 tsps ginger, chopped, 3 dry red chillies, 1 tsp coriander seeds, 1 tsp cumin seeds, 4 cloves , ½ tsp turmeric, 6 whole pepper corns, — dry roasted in a tava and then ground with little water.

½ cup tomato, chopped
2 tbsps yoghurt
2 green cardamoms, crushed
2 tsps salt
Water
Ghee or oil

* Mix in a bowl ground jackfruit, gram flour, soda, salt and coconut chilli paste. Knead well and shape into small rounds.
* Heat ghee or oil in a pan and deep fry jackfruit balls until all sides turn brown. Drain well and keep aside.
* Heat ghee or oil in another pan and fry onions and garlic until golden. Add ginger and ground spices, fry again until oil begins to separate.
* Add tomatoes, yoghurt, cardamoms and salt, stir well and fry for few minutes more. Add enough hot water to make a gravy. Cover and cook for further 10 minutes.
* Add the fried koftas, lower heat and cook for 7-8 minutes over low flame.
* Serve hot garnished with coriander leaves.

Cooking time: 35 minutes   To serve: 4-6

Sarson da Saag

Delicacy of Punjab

1 kg mustard greens, cleaned,
washed and chopped
250 gms bathuway or spinach
leaves, cleaned and washed
2 medium onions, finely sliced
6 cloves garlic
1″ piece fresh ginger, chopped
6 green chillies
2 tsps salt
2 level tbsps maize flour
1 tsp sugar
Water

For tadka
6 tbsps ghee
1″ piece fresh ginger, and
6 cloves garlic, ground

To garnish
4 green chillies, deseeded
and cut lengthways
2 tbsps white butter

☆ Place cut mustard greens and spinach in a heavy bottom pan with onion, garlic, ginger, chillies and salt. Add enough water and cook over low heat for 1½ hours.
☆ Remove from fire, add sugar and maize flour and grind to a smooth paste.
☆ Heat ghee and fry garlic and ginger until light brown in colour. Add ground mixture, stir for 10 minutes and remove from fire. Transfer to a serving bowl.
☆ Garnish with green chillies and white butter just before serving.
☆ Serve hot with makkai ki roti, chutney and lassi.

Cooking time: 2 hours   To serve: 4-6   Picture on page: 6

Pasanda Kabab

Kashmiri lamb kabab

½ kg lean boneless meat (from leg)
2" piece ginger, 6 cloves garlic,
2 medium onions and 6 peppercorns
— ground to a paste

1 tsp Kashmiri red chilli powder
3 tbsps raw papaya, grated

A pinch of asafoetida
1 tsp garam masala
100 gms oil or ghee

* Trim all the fat from the meat and cut into 3" slices and ½" thickness.
* Place them on a chopping board and beat lightly with a meat mallet on one side, to flatten. These are called pasandas.
* Add red chilli, garam masala, grated papaya, asafoetida and salt to the ground paste.
* Smear both the sides of the pasanda with this mixture and keep aside **for 2 hours**.
* Roll each pasanda and secure with a string.
* Heat oil or ghee in a heavy bottom pan and fry them over low heat.
* Place the pasanda under hot grill until colour become reddish brown.

Cooking time: 45 minutes   To serve: 4-6

Kaleji Kabab

250 gms liver, remove outer skin and
cut into 2" squares
½ cup (150 gms) yoghurt
cloves of garlic and 1" piece
ginger — ground to a paste

1 tsp garam masala
1 tsp coriander seeds powder
1 tsp cumin seeds powder
½ tsp Kashmiri red chilli powder
1 tsp salt

1 tbsp lime juice
1 tbsp oil
Extra oil for basting
Few wedges of lime and raw
onion for garnishing

Mix together ground ginger-garlic paste and yoghurt. Add all remaining spices, lime juice and mix thoroughly.

Wash and pat the liver dry. Mix well with yoghurt mixture and set aside **for 6 hours.**

Arrange the liver squares on skewers. Cook in a 'Rotisserie' or grill, basting frequently with ghee or oil, till the liver is tender.

Garnish with lime wedges and onion rings.

Serve hot with mint chutney and rotis.

Cooking time: 20 minutes   To serve: 4

Galavat ke Kabab

Kashmiri griddle kabab

500 gms mince meat (lamb or beef)
100 gms bengal gram
2 medium onions, grated
3 tbsps raw papaya, grated

6 peppercorns
2 large cardamoms, shelled
1 tsp coriander seeds
2 level tsps salt

1 level tsp Kashmiri red chilli
powder (optional)
4 cloves
Oil for shallow frying

* Boil mince meat with little salt until soft. Put in a blender for a minute.
* Dry roast and grind cardamoms, coriander, cloves and bengal gram, each separately. Add to the minced meat. Add only half of the bengal gram.
* Grind together papaya, pepper and onion. Make a paste and add salt and chilli powder.
* Add masala paste to the minced mixture, knead well, cover and keep aside **for 2 hours**.
* Add remaining bengal gram making the kababs. Knead well again.
* Heat a griddle. Put little oil. Place a small portion of minced mixture, pressing them flat with fingers, fry until brown on both sides. Add a little oil each time before placing the minced mixture.

Note: These kababas are very soft — need to be handled carefully.

Cooking time: 25-30 minutes   To serve: 4-6

Peshawari Kabab

Fried mutton kababs Peshawari style

500 gms minced meat
2 medium size onions, grated
2 green chillies, seeded and chopped
½ tsp black pepper powder
1 tsp poppy seeds

1 tsp cumin seeds, roasted and ground
2 tsps ginger, grated
1½ tsps salt
1 tbsp coriander leaves
1 egg, beaten

4 tbsps bread crumbs
6 lemon wedges
2½ cups (575 ml) water
Oil for deep frying

☆ Mix together minced meat, onions, chillies, pepper, cumin, poppy seeds, salt, ginger, coriander. Grind and make into a smooth dough.

☆ Divide the mince mixture into 8-10 parts. Put 2 or 3 tbsps of mixture in your palm then close your fist lightly to form an oblong shape kabab.

☆ Boil water, place the kababs. Simmer over low heat until all the water evaporates. Carefully remove the kababs into a plate.

☆ Heat oil in a shallow pan. Dip each kabab into the beaten egg, coat with crumbs and fry until both the sides become light brown.

☆ Serve with lemon wedges, onion and cucumber salad and rotis.

Cooking time: 30 minutes   To serve: 4-6

169

Hussaini Kabab

Skewered barbecued lamb

900 gms boneless lean meat, mutton or lamb
6 cloves garlic
1" piece ginger
1 tsp ground cumin seeds
1 tsp ground coriander seeds

2 level tsps salt
1 tsp black pepper, freshly ground
1 tbsp lemon juice
3 tbsps yoghurt
2 tbsps oil
½ tsp chilli powder

For topping
4 tbsps butter
150 ml milk
25 gms almonds or cashewnuts
100 gms cream

* Cut the meat into 1" (2.5 cms) cubes and put into a large bowl.
* Combine all ingredients and mix well. Marinate cut meat cubes in the mixture. Cover and leave **for 3-4 hours.**
* Thread 4 to 5 pieces of meat on each skewer and cook on a charcoal fire or under a pre-heated grill until crisp and brown all over.
* Grind almonds or cashewnuts to a fine paste.
* Melt butter, add milk, almond paste and cream and cook over a slow fire until mixture thickens.
* Place cooked kababs in a serving dish and spread the milk sauce over each kakab.
* Serve hot with parathas or naans.

Cooking time: 30 minutes

To serve: 4-6

Facing Page
Clockwise:

Shami Kabab
Murgh Makhani
Sheer-Mal
Mixed Vegetable Raita

Kabab Jahangiri

Minced lamb kababs with capsicum, tomatoes, onions and oriental spices

)0 gms minced lamb meat
medium onions, grated, 2 tbsps
w papaya, grated, 6 cloves garlic,
tsp cumin seeds, ½ tsp turmeric
owder, 2 tsps grated ginger, 1 tsp
aram masala, 2 green chillies,
eeded and chopped and 2 level
ps salt — ground to a smooth
aste

6 medium tomatoes, halved
2 capsicums, cut into bite size
2 large onions, cut into bite size

2 tbsps coriander leaves,
finely chopped
6 tbsps oil

Mince the meat twice. Combine together with 3 tbsps oil and ground masala. Mix well.
Divide the mixture between 6 skewers and use one portion of mixture on each skewer
and shape into long sausages. Smear oil.
Cook over glowing coal or under pre-heated griller, until browned on both sides.
Remove from skewer, cut into 3″ (7.5 mm) long pieces.
Heat remaining oil, saute onions, tomatoes and capsicums for 2 minutes, add cut
kababas. Stir well.
Serve hot with Naans, onion and lemon slices.

ooking time: 30 minutes   To serve: 4-6

:ing Page
)ckwise:

dey ki Roti
ti Kabab
matar ki Chutney
ansakh
uslim Naan
hudi Roti
irgh Jal Frazie (centre)
ya ki Nihari

Boti Kabab

1 kg boneless meat, preferably lamb
250 gms yoghurt
2″ piece of ginger, and 8 cloves
garlic — ground to a paste
1 tbsp vinegar
2 tbsps lemon juice
5 dry Kashmiri red chillies, ground to
a paste

8 cardamoms, powdered
8 cloves, powdered
10 whole peppercorns, powdered
1 tbsp poppy seeds and 1 tbsp
cashewnuts, ground together
2 tbsps oil
2 tsps salt

Lemon slice, cut radishes,
sauted crisp vegetables (onion
rings, capsicum rings) for
garnishing

For smoking
12 Cloves
Few pieces of live charcoal
1 tpsp ghee

* Cut meat into cubes approximately 1½″ in size.
* Mix rest of the ingredients in a bowl.
* Add meat cubes, mix well, marinate **for 10-12 hours.**
* Arrange the meat cubes on skewers. Cook on a charcoal fire or 'Rotisserie' till the meat is tender.
* Place the live charcoal in a small bowl or 'katori'. Place it in the middle of a large pre-heated pan with lid.
* Remove the boti kababs from the skewers and arrange around the bowl with charcoal. Now put the cloves over the coals, pour ghee on top and quickly cover with a lid. Smoke for 3-5 minutes and uncover.
* Garnish with lemon slices, cut radishes, spring onions, and sauted vegetables. Serve hot.

Cooking time: 15-20 minutes | To serve: 4 | Picture on page: 17:

Shami Kabab

50 gms finely minced meat
medium onions, chopped
tbsps yellow split peas or red lentil
tsp cardamom seeds
tsps garlic, finely chopped and
tsps ginger finely grated
– ground together

50 gms coriander leaves
3 green chillies
2 tsps salt
1 tsp garam masala
1 tsp cumin seeds powder
2½ cups (575 ml) water

Oil for shallow frying
2 eggs
1 lemon
Coriander leaves, finely
chopped

Boil minced meat with split peas or dal, cardamom seeds and salt, until the meat turns soft and almost dry.

Grind all ingredients together with boiled minced meat except oil and eggs.

Add eggs and mix well and knead for 10-15 minutes, until mixture is very smooth. Add juice of one lemon and coriander leaves.

Divide the mixture into 8-10 portions and shape into flat rounds ½" thick, 3" (7.5 cms) diameter.

Heat oil and shallow fry the kababs 2-3 at a time until both the sides are golden brown. Serve with pudina chutney.

Note: Traditionally this kabab is stuffed with finely chopped onions, green chillies and mashed hard boiled eggs before shaping it into flat rounds. Tastes excellent if prepared with this stuffing.

ooking time: 30 minutes   To serve: 4-6   Picture on page: 171

Lucknowi Korma

½ kg lean lamb
6 tbsps plain yoghurt
3 medium onions, chopped
3 cloves garlic
2 dry Kashmiri chillies, seeded
2 tbsps fresh ginger, grated
16 almonds, blanched

2 tsps poppy seeds
1 tsp cumin seeds, ground
1 tsp peppercorns, coarsely ground
3 large black cardamoms
3 small green cardamoms, crushed

6 strands saffron
2 tbsps hot water
3 tbsps fresh coriander leaves,
finely chopped
Ghee or oil

* Trim off fat and cut meat into large cubes. Wash and drain.
* Place a piece of muslin over a small bowl and spoon the yoghurt into it, tie ends securely and hang to drain over the bowl.
* Pound saffron strands and then dissolve in hot water.
* Keep one chopped onion aside. Put 2 chopped onions, garlic, ginger, dry chillies and almonds in a blender or food processor and blend to a smooth paste. Then add poppy seeds, cumin and peppercorns, blend for a few seconds more.
* Heat 4 tbsps melted ghee or oil. Fry the remaining onion, stirring frequently. Fry to a pale golden colour. Add both the cardamoms, meat and salt. Stirring constantly fry the meat for 10 minutes to a rich brown colour. The ghee will start to separate at this stage.
* Add the blended mixture and fry for 10 minutes stirring all the time. Rinse out blender container with ¼ cup of water and add to pan. Stir until the gravy dries up again. Continue stirring and frying until the mixture is well browned.
* Add drained yoghurt 1 tbsp at a time and stirring continuously, fry until the ghee once again begins to separate.
* Pour 2½ cups of hot water. Stir well. Cover the lid and cook over low flame until the meat is tender and the gravy has thickened.
* Sprinkle with coriander leaves. Serve hot.

Cooking time: 1 hour 45 minutes   To serve: 4-6   Picture on page: 22

Gosht Do Piaza

A Mughlai dish of meat for those who enjoy onions

½ kg meat shoulder or hind leg of lamb
1 kg onions, 2 finely sliced and rest finely chopped
150 ml plain yoghurt, beaten
2 level tsps ground coriander
½ level tsp turmeric powder

1 level tsp chilli powder
1½ level tsps salt
3 cloves garlic, crushed
1″ piece fresh ginger, finely chopped
5 cloves

2 bay leaves
1 tbsp lemon juice
1 level tsp garam masala
Ghee or oil

* Cut the meat into large cubes 1½″ (4 cms).
* Heat 1 tbsp ghee or oil in a heavy bottom pan. Spread half of the chopped onions on the bottom.
* Place the meat over it, sprinkle with ground coriander, yoghurt, chilli powder, turmeric and salt and cover the surface with remaining onions and sprinkle water on top. Cover the pan with a tight fitting lid and simmer gently over low flame for 1 hour until the onions are reduced to a pulp and the meat is tender.
* Scrape the sides of the pan and stir well.
* Heat 4 tbsps ghee or oil in a separate pan. Fry sliced onions until pale golden. Add garlic, ginger, bay leaves and cloves. Stirring frequently, fry for few minutes. Add 1 tbsp water and fry until the colour turns rich golden brown.
* Add the meat and onion mixture. Mix the ingredients, stirring frequently. Fry the mixture until it is well browned and a thick gravy has formed.
* Add lemon juice and garam masala, mix well, and fry for a few minutes more.
* Serve hot. Sprinkle with coriander leaves.

Note: The term — 'Do piaza' means using twice the weight of onions to meat but the dish was named originally after a minister of the Emperor Akbar, Mullah Do-piaza.

Cooking time: 1½ hours   To serve: 4-6

Paya ki Nihari

Trotters curry is a speciality of Goa and Bombay

6 trotters (paya), cleaned
4 black cardamoms, 1" stick
cinnamon and 4 cloves, slightly
crushed
1 level tsp fennel seeds
¼ tsp nutmeg
2 red dry chillies, seeded and cut
lengthways
1 level tsp turmeric powder
1 level tsp cumin seeds
1 level tbsp coriander seeds

8 cloves garlic
1" piece fresh ginger
2 bay leaves
4 tbsps tamarind pulp
(see page 20)
2 green chillies, finely cut
4 tbsps oil
2 level tsps salt

2 level tbsps wheat flour
2 level tbsps ghee
½ cup water

For garnishing
3 onions, fried crisp and
crushed
Mint leaves, chopped

☆ Wash the trotters well, cover them with boiling water. Scrape off hair with a knife. Then boil in salted water with bay leaves until tender.

☆ Grind red chillies, turmeric, coriander, cumin, fennel seeds, nutmeg, ginger and 6 cloves of garlic. Make a fine paste.

☆ Mince remaining 2 cloves of garlic.

☆ Heat oil in a pan. Fry garlic, cardamoms, cloves, cinnamon and the ground paste. Stir and fry until brown.

☆ Put in the trotters along with the water in which they have been boiled. Cover the lid. Simmer over low flame till almost dry.

☆ Saute the flour in ghee till it changes colour. Add ½ cup water, stir and simmer for 5 minutes. Add to the trotters.

☆ Add tamarind and salt. Mix well. Add green chillies. Add water if necessary, simmer again for 20 minutes. Garnish with fried crisp onions crushed and mint leaves.

Cooking time: 1 hour   To serve: 4-6   Picture on page: 172

Roghan Josh

1 kg meat (boned leg of lamb), cut
into cubes
1 cup (275 gms) yoghurt, beaten
100 gms khoya (dried milk) (see
page 17)
2" piece ginger, ground
4 cloves

A pinch of asafoetida
1 tsp Kashmiri red chilli powder
1 tsp soonth
2 (1") pieces cinnamon
1 tsp sugar
2 tsps Kashmiri garam masala (see
page 19)

A pinch of saffron
25 gms almonds, soaked and
blanched
1 tsp kewda water
250 gms ghee or oil
2½ tsps salt
2½ cups (575 ml) water

* Heat oil in a heavy bottom pan, over low heat. Add the asafoetida, ground ginger, cloves, cinnamon, soonth and chilli powder. Fry for 5 minutes and add meat.
* Simmer for 45 minutes until a reddish sediment begins to appear. Add 3-4 tbsps water and simmer again. Keep stirring continuously and scrape the sediment with a spatula.
* Cook until meat turns reddish brown in colour.
* Uncover the pan and increase the heat to moderate. Add sugar and half the water. When it has been absorbed, add remaining water.
* Cover and simmer for another 20 minutes. Add garam masala, saffron and make a paste with kewda water. Cover and simmer for another 10-15 minutes.
* Grind the khoya, yoghurt and almonds to a paste and add to the meat. Mix thoroughly and cook over low heat until the khoya turns brown.
* There should be very little gravy left.

Cooking time: 1½ hours   To serve: 4-6   Picture on page: 154

179

Kashmiri Kofta

½ kg minced meat
2 level tsps salt, 1 level tsp Kashmiri chilli powder, ½ level tsp dry ginger powder, 1 level tsp coriander powder, 3 tbsps plain yoghurt, 1 level tsp cumin seeds, 1 level tsp garam masala, 2 tbsps mustard oil, and 1" piece ginger, ground
— mix and keep aside

2 tbsps fresh coriander leaves, finely chopped
100 gms khoya (dried milk) (see page 17)
4 tbsps of arrowroot or gram flour
2½ cups (575 ml) plain yoghurt
4 tbsps melted ghee or oil
4 cloves

4 big cardamoms
1 level tsp salt
A pinch of asafoetida
4 strands of saffron, pounded and soaked in 2 tbsps milk
1 tsp kewda essence

* Combine in a bowl the minced meat and all the mixed ingredients well. Add khoya and arrowroot. Knead well.
* Heat ghee in a large heavy bottom pan. Add asafoetida, cloves and cardamoms.
* Add yoghurt and ½ cup of water and salt. Reduce heat and allow it to simmer.
* Take a tbsp of mince mixture and roll into a 2"-3" (5 cms-7½ cms) oblong and ¾" thick. Roll the dough with your palm over a metal plate.
* Slip each kofta carefully into the pan. Shake the container from time to time to prevent the koftas from sticking to the bottom. Scrape the sediment gently from the vessel with a spatula. Add 2 tbsps more water if it starts sticking to the pan.
* Cook till koftas change colour. Add 2½ cups of water. Cover and cook for 40 minutes. When the gravy thickens remove from fire. Sprinkle coriander leaves.
* Add saffron solution and kewda essence.

Note: Add 6-8 tbsps cream to the gravy if you want a richer texture.

Cooking time: 1 hour   To serve: 4-6

Gushtaba

Kashmiri meat balls in spicy yoghurt sauce

½ kg minced meat
½ tsps Kashmiri red chilli powder
level tsps ground coriander
owder
level tsp cumin seeds

3 level tsps salt
4 tbsps arrowroot
1 cup (250 gms) plain yoghurt, beaten
1 tsp sugar

1" piece fresh ginger, ground
2 tbsps coriander leaves, finely chopped
Ghee or oil
Water

- Add chilli powder, coriander, cumin, arrowroot and half the salt to the washed and dried kheema. Knead well and then form into firm round balls about the size of an egg.
- Heat enough ghee or oil to deep fry the meat balls. Fry 2 or 3 at a time until the colour turns golden brown. Drain and place them on a kitchen paper.
  In a separate pan heat 4 tbsps ghee or oil. Add ginger, sugar and yoghurt. Pour in 3 cups of water. Bring to a boil, stirring constantly. Add remaining salt. Reduce heat and gently add fried meat balls. Simmer over very low heat for 20 minutes. Cover the lid and cook for another 15 minutes.
- Serve hot, garnished with coriander leaves.

Cooking time: 45 minutes　　　　　To serve: 4-6　　　　　Picture on page: 205

Gosht Akbari

This exotic dish was served for Emperor Akbar with saffron rice

1 kg boneless lamb meat, clean and cut into cubes
3 medium size onions, chopped
½ cup dates, chopped
½ cup apricots, stoned and washed
¼ cup clean large white raisins
2 tbsps brown sugar
½ cup ghee
4 cups water
2 level tsps salt
Rind of ½ lime, grated
1 piece cinnamon
¾ cup dried prunes, pitted
6-8 green chillies (optional)

☆ Cook chopped dates in a pan with water until dates soften. Press through a sieve to puree. Heat half of the ghee in a heavy pan and fry meat cubes until brown. Remove meat from the ghee and add remaining ghee.

☆ Add onions and cook for 5 minutes. Reduce heat and add 1 cup water, salt, cinnamon, lemon rind, and fried meat. Simmer for 20 minutes and add 1 cup water again. Cover an cook for another 25 minutes.

☆ Add puree with apricots, prunes, raisins and brown sugar. Stir well, add more water, if necessary. Cover and simmer for an hour until the meat is tender. Serve, garnished with green chillies slit lengthways.

| Cooking time: 2 hours | To serve: 4-6 | Picture on page: 6 |

Gosht ka Sufed Salan

1 kg mutton cutlet or chops
2 cups milk
2 tsps white pepper powder
8 cloves
10 cashewnuts, ground to a paste
2 pieces cinnamon
4 green cardamoms, crushed
2 tsps chilli powder
2 tsps garam masala
1 cup (200 gms) cream
1 tsp sugar
Ghee
Water

☆ Heat ghee in a heavy bottom pan. Add cloves, cardamoms, cinnamon, chilli powder, an meat. Stir well and fry till the meat is light brown. Add cashewnut paste. Mix well.

☆ Add sugar and 2-3 cups water, allow to simmer over medium heat until tender and dry.

☆ Add garam masala, pepper and very slowly pour in the milk, stirring constantly till well blended.
Now cook over low heat until the gravy turns reddish white. Add cream and mix well. Remove from fire and serve hot.

| Cooking time: 50 minutes | To serve: 4-6 |

Seekh Kabab ki Curry

) ready-made seekh kababs, each
Jt into two pieces

or the gravy
large tomatoes, chopped
onions, finely chopped
cloves garlic, crushed

5 green cardamoms, crushed
1 stick cinnamon
5 cloves
2 tsps chilli powder
4 green chillies, slited
½ tsp black cumin seeds

1 tsp garam masala
2 tbsps fresh coriander,
chopped
½ cup ghee or oil
2 cups hot water
½ cup cream and few slices of
tomatoes

Heat ghee, add onions and garlic. Fry until the colour turns brown, add cinnamon,
cardamoms, cloves, cumin seeds, green chillies, chilli powder and tomatoes. Stir well
and fry until oil starts to separate.
Add the seekh kababs and salt. Stir gently, add water, cover and simmer for a few
minutes. Sprinkle garam masala and stir. Pour in the cream just before serving.
Remove from fire, place in a serving bowl, garnish with coriander leaves and tomato
slices.

ooking time: 25 minutes   To serve: 4-6

Dahiwale Chaap

kg lamb or mutton chops, washed
cups (500 ml) yoghurt
medium onions, 10 cloves garlic,
piece ginger, 4 dry chillies
ground together
evel tsps salt

2 level tsps roasted cumin powder
2 level tsps coriander powder
½ tsp pepper
1 level tsp onion seeds (kalonji)

½ cup tomato pulp
1 tsp garam masala
Ghee
4 tbsps coriander leaves,
finely chopped for garnishing

Mix together chops, yoghurt and onion paste.
Add remaining spices except tomato pulp and ghee. Mix well and keep aside **for 6 hrs.**
Heat ghee, add meat with the marinade and tomato pulp.
Stir well and cook for 10 to 15 minutes. Cover the lid and cook over low heat until meat is
tender and the gravy is almost dry. Garnish with coriander leaves.
Remove from fire and serve hot.

ooking time: 45-50 minutes   To serve: 4-6

Sultani Chops

Hyderabad

1 kg mutton chops
1 cup yoghurt
4 tbsps vinegar
3 medium onions, ½ cup raw papaya
and 8 cloves garlic — ground
together

2 tsps ginger juice
2 tsps garam masala
½ tsp black pepper
1 level tsp salt

2 level tsps chilli powder
Ghee
White of 2 eggs
Bread crumbs

* ★ Wash and flatten the chops
* ★ Mix onion-garlic paste, garam masala, chilli powder, vinegar, yoghurt, salt and pepper.
* ★ Add chops into the mixture and rub well on both sides, and set aside **for 3 hours**.
* ★ Beat the egg white lightly.
* ★ Drain each chop well and dip each piece in the beaten egg white, and coat with bread crumbs.
* ★ Heat ghee in a shallow pan and fry until golden brown. Serve hot.

Cooking time: 45 minutes   To serve: 4-6

Malai Gosht

kg boneless meat, cut into cubes
cups (1 litr) milk
cups (½ ltr) cream
eggs
medium onions, sliced

8 cloves garlic, 6 green chillies and
1″ piece ginger — ground together
20 almonds, blanched and sliced
6 tbsps raisins, soaked and sliced

1 tbsp butter
2 tbsps sugar
2 level tsps salt
Ghee

Heat ghee and fry ¼ of the sliced onions, ground spices, sugar and meat. Stir well, add salt and fry until light brown. Add enough water to cover. Simmer until meat is tender and a little gravy remains.

Add milk and cook again over medium heat until the quantity of milk is reduced to half. Fry the remaining sliced onions until light brown and mix with raisins and almonds.

Butter a round pan and spread a layer of meat then a layer of fried onion mixture then a layer of cream. Repeat these three layers and end with the onion mixture.

Slowly break the eggs carefully on top of the layer of onion mixture (do not break the yolk).

Bake in a moderately hot oven until eggs are well set. Serve hot.

ooking time: 1 hour   To serve: 4-6

Gosht Hyderabadi

1 kg boneless meat
2½ cups yoghurt, beaten well
2 large onions, sliced
1" piece ginger, chopped

12 cloves garlic, chopped
6 dry chillies
½ tsp turmeric powder
4 cardamoms

2 pieces cinnamon
6 cloves
Ghee
½ cup flour

☆ Heat ghee, add chillies, onions, garlic, ginger, cardamoms, cinnamon and cloves. Stir well. Add meat and mix well.

☆ Mix turmeric with the yoghurt and add to the meat. Stir well and fry for a few minutes.

☆ Make a thick paste with flour and water.

☆ Cover the pan with a tight lid and put a weight on top. Seal it with flour paste and cook over low heat for 45 minutes.

☆ Remove the cover. Stir well and add more ghee and fry uncovered until meat is reddish brown. Remove from fire and serve hot.

Cooking time: 1 hour 10 minutes   To serve: 4-6

Kamargagh

Kashmir

2 cutlets of lamb with 1 rib each
cups (½ lt) milk
peppercorns
tsp aniseeds
green cardamoms

1 small stick cinnamon
5 cloves
4 tbsps gram flour (optional)
4 tbsps rice flour

1 level tsp salt
2½ tsps chilli powder
A pinch of asafoetida
1 cup ghee

In a piece of thin cloth place peppercorns, aniseeds, cardamoms, cinnamon, cloves, and tie them together.

In a large pan place together meat, milk, spices and 2½ cups of water. Boil for 25 minutes till the meat becomes tender and the liquid evaporates.

Mix gram flour, rice flour, water together and make a batter. Beat until it acquires a light consistency. To test the batter, drop a tsp of it into a cup of water. If the batter floats the consistency is correct, if not beat again.

Add chilli, asafoetida and salt to the batter and beat well.

Heat the ghee, dip the pieces of meat in the batter and fry until golden brown.

If you do not wish to use gram flour, then dip the meat pieces in the remaining milk, coat with rice flour and fry.

Serve hot.

Cooking time: 50 minutes   To serve: 6

Rajasthani Hara Gosht

Meat cooked in spinach and mint juice without water

450 gms boneless, lean meat
450 gms spinach, clean and extract the juice
250 gms fresh mint leaves, extract the juice
1 cup (250 ml) plain yoghurt, beaten

4 medium onions, finely chopped
8 cloves garlic, 1" piece fresh ginger, 1 level tsp cumin seeds, 1 level tsp coriander seeds — ground to a paste
10 green chillies, seeded and washed

2 level tsps salt
Ghee or oil
1 large onion, sliced and rings separated

☆ Clean and wash the spinach and mint thoroughly. Extract the juice separately.
☆ Heat 4 tbsps ghee or oil, fry onions until brown. Add meat along with the ground paste. Stir and fry for few minutes. Add salt.
☆ Stir in yoghurt. Cover and cook over low flame for 30 minutes. Stir time to time.
☆ Pour in spinach and mint juices. Mix thoroughly. Cover the lid. Cook until meat is tender and the gravy dries up.
☆ Serve hot garnished with onion rings and green chillies.

Cooking time: 1 hour	To serve: 4-6

Lassan

Minced meat with garlic and eggs, a Muslim speciality

250 gms minced meat
tbsps garlic, finely chopped
onion, grated, 1 tsp cumin seeds,
½ tsp black cumin seeds, 1 tsp
ginger, finely chopped, ½ tsp poppy
seeds, 2 green chillies, seeded and
chopped — ground to a smooth
paste

½ tsp turmeric powder
4 tomatoes, chopped
1 tbsp coriander, finely chopped
1½ tsps salt

½ tsp pepper
2 eggs beaten
8 tbsps oil
Hot water

Heat 4 tbsps oil, fry the ground masala paste, for 8-10 minutes. Add turmeric, tomatoes, pepper and fry till oil separates. Add minced meat, stir well and fry until colour turns brown. Pour hot water. Cover and simmer over low heat until done. The mince should be dry.

In a deep serving plate, cover the bottom of the plate with chopped garlic.
Spread the hot minced meat over it evenly.
Pour beaten eggs over it and sprinkle chopped coriander.

Heat remaining oil. Now drizzle piping hot oil all over the egg mixture. The heat of oil will immediately cook the egg mixture, binding the meat and garlic. Serve hot with freshly prepared thin chapatis.

Cooking time: 30 minutes | To serve: 4-6 | Picture on page: 68

Murgh Badami

Chicken dish of hundred almonds with gravy which was one of the favourite dishes of the Great Mughal Emperor, Akbar

1¼ kg chicken
100 gms almonds, blanched and ground
250 ml yoghurt
4 medium ripe tomatoes, blanched and chopped
3 medium onions, sliced thinly
8 cloves garlic, chopped

1 tbsp fresh ginger, finely grated
1 level tsp black cumin seeds, ground
1 level tsp coriander, ground
1 level tsp turmeric powder
½ level tsp fennel seeds, ground
1 level tsp chilli powder
2 level tsps salt

4 tbsps fresh mint leaves, finely chopped
8 small green cardamoms
Ghee or oil
Extra 10 almonds, blanched, slivered and fried golden

☆ Cut the chicken into 8 pieces.
☆ Heat 3 tbsps ghee or oil in a heavy based pan. Fry the chicken pieces and keep aside.
☆ Add another 3 tbsps ghee or oil and fry onions over low heat until tender pale golden in colour. Do not let them get brown as this will change the creamy colour of the sauce.
☆ Add garlic, ginger, cardamoms and all the ground spices. Stir for 2 minutes, add tomatoes, salt and half the mint. Cook over very low heat, stirring frequently.
☆ Add ½ cup water if the mixture sticks to the pan. Add chicken pieces. Stir and cover the lid, cook gently until the chicken is tender.
☆ Beat the yoghurt lightly with a fork and stir into the chicken mixture. Add almond paste. Stir well. Simmer for 10 minutes.
☆ Transfer to a serving dish. Sprinkle fried almonds and chopped mint.

Cooking time: 1 hour 20 minutes   To serve: 4-6   Picture on page: 6

Murgh Shahenshahi

A truly royal Mughlai recipe, chicken cooked with oriental spices, dried fruits and herbs

2 (total weight 2½ kgs) chickens
225 gms minced lamb
3 medium size onions, chopped
3 medium size tomatoes, chopped
8 cloves garlic, 2 tbsps fresh ginger, chopped and 6 Kashmiri red chillies — ground to a fine paste
1 tsp turmeric powder
3 tbsps poppy seeds, 3 tbsps broken cashewnuts — ground together

8 cardamoms
8 cloves
25 gms sultanas
5½ cups (1000 ml) water
75 gms ghee
2½ level tsps salt

For garnishing
4 eggs hard boiled, cut into half and shaped into a flower
4 small onions, sliced
2 tbsps beetroot juice or a few drops red colour
2 tbsps fried cashewnuts
2 tbsps coriander leaves, finely chopped

* Clean the chicken and cut into 4 or 6 joints
* Heat ghee, add onion and saute for 10 minutes.
* Add poppy seeds-cashewnuts paste. Stir well, fry for 8 minutes.
* Add half of the ginger-garlic paste. Fry, add half of the turmeric and tomatoes.
* Fry for 5-10 minutes more. Add cloves and cardamoms. If the mixture sticks to the bottom of the pan, sprinkle a little water.
* Add sultanas and chicken pieces. Pour water. Cover and cook over low heat till the chicken is done and gravy is thick.
* Cook minced lamb with remaining ginger-garlic-chilli paste, turmeric and tomatoes.
* Before serving arrange the chicken pieces on a bed of cooked minced lamb. Pour over the gravy.
* Garnish with egg flowers, arrange onion slices around the dish, sprinkle fried cashewnuts and beetroot juice and coriander leaves.

Cooking time: 1 hour   To serve: 4-6

Murg Khubani

A classic chicken dish of Kashmir, cooked with dry apricots and aromatic spices

1 (kg) chicken, skinned
2 medium tomatoes, chopped
12 dried Kashmiri apricots, **soaked overnight** and stoned
3 medium onions, finely sliced
6 cloves garlic, finely sliced

2 tbsps fresh ginger, grated
3 green chillies, seeded and chopped
3 small cardamom pods, crushed
1" stick cinnamon
6 strands saffron

2 tbsps hot milk or water
2 level tsps salt
2 cups (425 ml) water
2 tsps kewda water
Ghee or oil

* Cut the chicken into 8 pieces.
* Drain apricots and remove stones.
* Heat 3 tbsps melted ghee or oil. Fry onion, garlic, ginger, chillies, cardamoms, cinnamon, until onions are golden brown in colour.
* Add tomatoes and salt along with chicken pieces. Fry for few minutes stirring frequently until oil separates. Pour in the water. Cover the lid tightly and reduce heat. Simmer over low heat for 25 minutes.
* Pound the saffron and dissolve in hot milk or water.
* Add apricots and saffron solution to the pan. Stir well. Cover again. Cook another 10 minutes over low heat. Stir carefully. Apricots should not become mushy.
* Remove from fire and sprinkle kewda water.

Cooking time: 45 minutes   To serve: 4-6

Murgh Korma Qutub Shahi

1 (1¼ kg) chicken, skinned and cut into 8 pieces
1 cup (250 gms) plain yoghurt
2 medium onions, finely sliced
1 1" stick cinnamon
3 small cardamoms, crushed
5 cloves
2 bay leaves

2 medium onions, chopped
4 green chillies, seeded and chopped, 10 cloves garlic, chopped, 1 tbsp ginger, finely grated, 6 tbsps grated fresh coconut or desiccated
1 level tbsp poppy seeds, ½ level tsp turmeric powder, 1 tbsp coriander, finely chopped — ground to a fine paste

2 level tsps salt
2 tbsps raisins or sultanas, washed
Juice of one lemon
1¼ cups (275 ml) water
4 tbsps ghee or oil
1 tbsp coriander leaves, finely chopped

* Heat ghee or oil, fry the sliced onion until golden. Add cloves, cardamoms, cinnamon and bay leaves, fry for 1 or 2 minutes.
* Add ground paste. Stirring continuously, fry the mixture until well browned. Add chicken pieces, yoghurt, salt and raisins and stir well. Cover and simmer over low heat for 15-20 minutes.
* Pour in water. Stir well. Cover and cook again until the chicken is tender and gravy has thickened.
* Serve hot, garnished with coriander and lemon juice.

Cooking time: 1 hour   To serve: 4-6

Murgh Jal Frazie

Spicy dry fried chicken

1 (1¼ kg) chicken
3 medium onions, thinly sliced
2 level tsps chilli powder
½ cup (150 gms) plain yoghurt
beaten lightly
Ghee or oil
2 tbsps coriander leaves,
finely chopped

For marinade
4 tbsps plain yoghurt
4 cloves garlic, crushed
1 level tsp garam masala (see page 19)
1 level tsp coriander, ground
1 level tsp cumin seeds, ground
½ level tsp turmeric powder
2 tsps fresh ginger, finely grated
2½ level tsps salt

* ☆ Combine all marinade ingredients in a bowl and mix thoroughly.
* ☆ Cut chicken into 4 or 6 pieces. Rub marinade mixture well over the chicken pieces and set aside **for 6 hours.**
* ☆ Heat 6 tbsps ghee or oil in a heavy based pan. Fry onions until golden brown. Drain and place on a kitchen paper.
* ☆ In the same oil fry chicken pieces until both the sides are browned well. Add remaining marinade, chilli powder, and ½ cup of water.
* ☆ Reduce heat, cover the lid and simmer until tender.
* ☆ Stir in the yoghurt a little at a time. Add fried onions, cover and simmer again for 5-6 minutes. Serve hot garnished with coriander.

Cooking time: 45 minutes   To serve: 4-6   Picture on page: 172

Murgh Makhani

Charcoal grilled marinated spring chicken in butter sauce

2 (1 kg each) spring chickens, whole
250 gms yoghurt
1" piece ginger, 8 cloves garlic
— ground together
1¼ kg ripe tomatoes
4 sticks of cinnamon, 8 cloves, 8
cardamoms, 10 black peppercorns
— powdered together

1 tsp dry fenugreek leaves
1 tbsp white pepper powder
2 tbsps lime juice
2 tbsps cream
1 tsp red tandoori mix
500 gms butter
2 level tsps salt
1 tsp chilli powder

For garnishing
25 gms cashewnuts, fried
2 tbsps coriander leaves,
chopped

* Clean chickens and remove skin. **Do not cut into pieces.**
* Mix together yoghurt, tandoori mix, ginger-garlic paste, lime juice, powdered spices and salt. Rub chickens well with this mixture and marinate **for 6 hours or overnight** for best results.
* Place chickens in a heavy bottom pan and roast over a charcoal fire or in a pre-heated oven (250°F 130°C-Gas Mark) for 10-15 minutes until tender.
* Cut tomatoes into quarters. Put the tomatoes in a pan without water. Cook over low heat. Bring to a boil. Stir well, cook until the sauce has reduced to half. Strain through a fine sieve.
* Put the strained tomato sauce in a pan and add the butter to it. Season with white pepper, chilli powder, remaining salt and fenugreek leaves.
* Just before serving, add cream to the sauce.
* Cut the cooked chicken into 4 joints. Place them in a deep serving plate, pour the sauce over the chickens.
* Garnish with fried cashewnuts and coriander leaves.

Cooking time: 45 minutes   To serve: 4-6   Picture on page: 171

Murgh Noorjahani

Chicken legs with oriental gravy

6 chicken legs or drumsticks
4 tbsps yoghurt
1 large onion, finely chopped
4 cloves garlic, crushed
2 tbsps fresh ginger, finely chopped
½ tsp turmeric powder

1 tsp red chilli powder
3 tsps coriander, ground
1 tsp level salt
1 tbsp coriander leaves, finely chopped
1 tsp ground cumin seeds

2 tbsps raisins
1 tbsp broken cashewnuts
4 tbsps ghee or oil
1 large ripe tomato, chopped
2 cups (425 ml) water

☆ Prick the chicken legs all over, apply yoghurt and little crushed garlic on them, cover and keep aside **for 6 hours.**

☆ Heat ghee or oil, fry onion, garlic, ginger until light brown, add turmeric, cumin, chilli, coriander, raisins and cashewnuts. Fry for a few minutes and add tomato. Keep stirring and fry until oil floats on the surface.

☆ Add chicken legs, cook over low heat stirring constantly. When the gravy begins to stick to the sides, add water. Cover and cook over low heat until done. Sprinkle coriander leaves.

Cooking time: 30 minutes   To serve: 4-6

Bohri Murgh

Marinated whole chicken, deep fried

2 (½ kg each) chickens
½ cup + 4 tbsps (175 gms) yoghurt, highly beaten
6 cloves garlic, crushed
3 spring onions, chopped
2 tsps fresh ginger, finely grated
1 tsp cumin seeds, ground
2 tsps chilli powder

½ tsp pepper
1½ level tsps salt
2 tbsps lemon juice
2 tbsps coriander leaves, finely chopped
Oil for deep frying
Spring onions for garnishing

For batter
4 eggs
2 tbsps gram flour
½ tsp salt
½ tsp chilli powder

- Grind together, onion, garlic, ginger, coriander, cumin and lemon juice. Add salt, pepper, chilli, and yoghurt. Mix well.
- Cut each chicken in halves down the centre, now rub yoghurt mixture well into the chicken. Cover and **marinate overnight.**
- Place chicken in a pan and cook uncovered for 30 minutes.
- Beat eggs, add besan, salt and chilli powder. Beat again.
- Heat oil. Dip each chicken into the batter and deep fry until colour turns golden and crispy. Serve hot garnished with spring onions.

Note: For an extra crispy surface use rice flour. This is one of the specialities of the Bohri community of India.

Cooking time: 40 minutes   To serve: 4

197

Murgh Xaccuti

This is a classic dish of Goa cooked with special xaccuti masala

1 (1¼ kg) chicken, skinned and cut into 8 pieces
½ large fresh coconut, grated or
6 tbsps desiccated coconut
3 large onions, chopped
12 cloves garlic, 1″ piece ginger
— ground together

1½ level tsps salt
1 level tsp turmeric powder
Juice of 1 lemon
Ghee or oil
2½ cups (575 ml) water

For Xaccuti masala
6 Kashmiri dry chillies, seeded, 3 tsps coriander seeds, ½ tsp cumin seeds, 1 tsp fenugreek seeds, 2 tsps poppy seeds, 5 small cardamoms, shelled, 6 cloves, 1″ piece cinnamon — each roasted separately and ground together to a fine paste

* Rub thoroughly garlic paste and lemon juice to the chicken pieces and keep aside.
* Dry roast freshly grated or desiccated coconut in a griddle and grind together with rest of the roasted spices.
* Heat 4 tbsps ghee or oil. Fry onions until golden brown and add the ground masala. Stirring frequently fry until colour turns brown and add 1-2 tbsps water. Stir well.
* Add the marinated chicken, turmeric and salt, mix thoroughly. Fry for a few minutes, pour in the water and cover the lid. Reduce heat and simmer gently until the chicken is tender and the gravy has thickened (gravy should be thick).
* Sprinkle remaining lemon juice. Serve hot.

Cooking time: 50 minutes   To serve: 4-6

Murg Raiwali

Chicken curry with mustard

(1 kg each) chickens cut, washed ～d drained
medium size onions, peeled and ～opped
green chillies, slit lengthways

2 green chillies, 1 whole pod garlic, 1 medium size onion, 2″ piece ginger, 6 curry leaves, 2 tbsps mustard seeds, cleaned, soaked and washed, or 2-3 tbsps ready-made mustard powder — ground to a paste with half of the vinegar

1 cup vinegar
1 tsp black pepper
6 cloves
1 tsp chilli powder
2 tsps salt
¾ cup ghee or oil
2 cups water

Place the chicken and ground paste together in a bowl, mix well and marinate **for 2 hours.**

Heat ghee or oil in a large heavy pan over medium heat. Add cloves and chopped onions and cook until the onions are browned.

Add the marinated chicken, salt, pepper, chilli powder, vinegar water. Cook over low heat for 45 minutes or until chicken is tender. Add green chillies. Serve hot.

ɔoking time: 1 hour   To serve: 4-6

Konkan Murgh

2 medium size chickens, cleaned and cut into small pieces
1 fresh coconut, grated
1 tsp cumin seeds
4 large tomatoes, chopped
3 large onions, chopped

1" piece ginger, grated
4 green chillies, chopped
A pinch of turmeric powder
2 tsps vinegar
2 tsps salt

10 whole peppercorns
2 red chillies
8 cloves
1 small piece cinnamon
½ cup ghee

* Grind coconut with cumin and turmeric powder and extract the milk twice.
* Heat ghee, add peppercorns, red chillies, cloves, cinnamon, 2 tbsps of ground coconut and fry for 2-3 minutes. Then add onions, green chillies, ginger and fry for 5-6 minutes. Add tomatoes and fry till oil separates. Add vinegar and the cut chicken pieces. Stir well and fry.
* Add half the coconut milk, cook over low heat until dry.
* Add remaining coconut milk, bring to a boil, cook till the chicken is done and the gravy is thick. Remove from heat and serve hot.

Cooking time: 45 minutes   To serve: 4-6   Picture on page: 12

Rubian Tandoori

Tandoori prawns

2 kg Bombay king size prawns, cleaned and divided
tbsps plain yoghurt, lightly beaten
cloves garlic, ground

1 tbsp fresh ginger, finely grated
6 tbsps lemon juice
½ tsp garam masala
½ tsp pepper

2 tsps cumin seeds, roasted and ground
1 tsp salt
1 tsp tandoori colour powder
4 tbsps extra oil

Add ginger, garlic, lemon juice, salt, 2 tbsps oil, pepper, cumin powder, garam masala and food colour to the yoghurt, stir well. Keep aside for 20 minutes.
If you are using king size prawns, then cut them into 2 or 3 pieces. Add the prawns to the yoghurt and mix well. Cover and set aside for 45 minutes.
Thread 4 to 5 pieces of prawns on each skewer, dip in oil. Cook over glowing coals or under a pre-heated griller, until crisp and brown all over, turning once or twice.
Serve hot.

Cooking time: 1 hour   To serve: 4-6   Picture on page: 67

Bombay Jhinga Bhajia

Prawn fritters Bombay style

50 gms Bombay prawns, deveined, washed and drained
tbsps (heaped) gramflour (besan)
small onion, finely grated
cloves garlic, crushed

1 tsp ginger, finely grated
½ tsp salt
1 tsp coriander leaves, finely chopped
¼ tsp pepper

½ tsp cumin powder
1 cup water
Oil for deep frying

Since Bombay prawns are king size, cut them into bite size pieces.
Mix in a large bowl gramflour, onion, garlic, ginger, salt, coriander leaves, pepper, cumin powder with water. Beat well with a wooden spoon.
Heat oil and when a faint haze appears over the surface, dip few pieces of prawns at a time in the besan mixture and deep fry over low flame until golden brown.
Drain on a kitchen paper and serve hot with pudina chutney or tomato sauce.

Cooking time: 30 minutes   To serve: 4-6

Madras Tisrya Masala

Spicy mussels Madras style

2 lbs (1 kg) fresh mussels
2 large onions, finely chopped
6 cloves garlic, finely chopped
3 tsps fresh ginger, finely chopped

2 dry Kashmiri red chillies, seeded
and chopped
½ tsp turmeric powder
2 tsps coriander powder
½ tsp salt

2 tbsps coriander leaves,
finely chopped
3 tbsps lemon juice
1¼ cups (275 ml) water
4 tbsps oil

* Clean mussels (scrub well and beard them).
* Heat oil, fry onions, garlic and ginger over medium heat until onions are golden.
* Add turmeric, coriander powder, chillies and fry for 3 minutes. Add water and salt, bring to a boil. Cover and cook for 5 minutes.
* Add mussels. Cover and simmer for 15 minutes until the shells have opened. Remove from heat. Place them on a deep plate.
* Sprinkle coriander leaves and lemon juice and spoon the gravy over and into the mussel shells. Serve hot.

Note: Discard any mussel if it did not open during cooking.

Cooking time: 30 minutes   To serve: 4-6

Lobster Khaibari

A Bombay delicacy

lbs (1 kg) large lobsters
medium onions, finely chopped
medium tomatoes, blanched and
hopped
cloves garlic, 1″ piece fresh ginger,
tbsps desiccated coconut, 1 tsp
oppy seeds, and 2 green chillies,
eeded — ground to a smooth paste

1 level tsp ground coriander
1 level tsp ground cumin
½ level tsp ground black pepper
½ level tsp turmeric powder
1 level tsp chilli powder
1 level tsp salt
1 level tsp garam masala (see page
19)

2 tbsps coriander leaves,
finely chopped
2 tbsps plain yoghurt
4 tbsps vegetable oil
Water

Carefully remove the meat from the lobsters' shell and wash well.
Heat oil in a pan over medium heat and fry onions until pale brown. Add the garlic paste, stir and fry till golden brown.
Add tomatoes, mix well. Fry stirring continuously for few minutes until the oil begins to separate.
Add coriander, cumin, pepper, chilli powder, turmeric and salt. Stir well, add the lobster meat and yoghurt. Fry for a few minutes and pour in ½ cup of water. Cover tightly. Reduce heat. Simmer over a low heat until the meat is tender. Add a little more water if necessary. Sprinkle garam masala. Stir well.
Serve hot, garnished with coriander.

ooking time: 30 minutes   To serve: 4-6

Malabar Machhi Molee

A classic fish dish of South India

2 pomfrets (½ kg each) or any other fish
3 medium onions, finely chopped
2 pieces fresh ginger, finely grated
5 green chillies, seeded and finely chopped
½ tsp cumin seeds

½ fresh coconut, grated (or 2½ cups desiccated coconut)
¼ tsp turmeric powder
4 medium tomatoes, blanched and chopped
1 tsp vinegar

1 tbsp lemon juice
1½ level tsps salt
3 tbsps ghee or vegetable oil
1 medium tomato, sliced thinly
1 medium onion, sliced thinly

* Clean, wash and cut fish into fillets or steaks (do not remove bones).
* Grind the coconut with turmeric and cumin seeds. Extract the milk twice (with little water the second time).
* Heat ghee or oil in a pan. Add chopped onions and ginger and ground coconut. Fry for a minute or two. Add tomatoes and chillies and fry over very low heat (do not allow any of the ingredients to brown). Cook for 5 minutes, stirring frequently.
* Add second extract of coconut milk and stir. When it comes to simmering point, add the fish and cook gently uncovered for 10 minutes.
* Add the thick coconut milk (the first extract). Stir gently.
* Add salt and vinegar, simmer over low heat for few minutes and remove from heat. Add thinly sliced onion and tomato. Sprinkle lemon juice.

Note: 'Fish Molee' is a speciality of South India (Kerala). Traditionally served with fluffy rice as main dish for lunch or dinner. 'Molee' can be made with chicken or lamb also.

Cooking time: 45 minutes	To serve : 4-6

Facing Page
Clockwise:

Kashmiri Roti Takta
Hari Roti
Gushtaba
Mahi Dum Kashmiri
Mewa Rasedar
Angoor ki Lassi
Mithi Laal Roti

Mahi Dum Kashmiri

A classic fish dish of Kashmir, cooked in yoghurt sauce and aromatic spices

pomfrets (½ kg each) or any other
sh
" piece fresh ginger, finely grated
pinch of asafoetida
½ level tsp cumin seeds
tbsps plain yoghurt

2 level tsps Kashmiri garam masala
(see page 19)
1½ level tsps ground coriander
1½ level tsps salt
4 sprigs of fresh coriander leaves,
finely chopped

4 green chillies, seeded and
sliced
Ghee or vegetable oil
Water

Clean and wash fish and cut into fillets or steaks. Rub little salt and turmeric. Keep aside for 10 minutes.

Heat ghee or oil in a large fry pan. Fry fish pieces lightly until pale golden, drain and place on kitchen paper.

Heat 3 tbsps melted ghee or oil in a heavy based pan. Add asafoetida, cumin, ginger and as they pop and splutter, pour in the yoghurt. Cook over low heat, stirring frequently until the colour turns reddish brown.

Add the fried fish pieces along with ground coriander and 1 cup of water. Cover the lid tightly. Simmer over low heat for 15 minutes until the gravy has thickened slightly.

Add garam masala, chopped coriander and chillies. Mix well. Cover again tightly. Cook for another 8-10 minutes or cover with a foil, then fix the lid and bake in a pre-heated oven (180°C-350°F-Gas mark 4) for 10 minutes.

Transfer to a serving dish. Serve hot.

| ooking time: 50 minutes | To serve: 4-6 | Picture on page: 205 |

Patra ni Machhi

A classic Parsi fish dish cooked in banana leaf

2 pomfrets (½ kg each) or small
sole, cut into fillets
3 level tsps salt
3 tbsps lemon juice
Banana leaves or foil

For chutney
10 tbsps fresh coriander, finely
chopped
1 fresh coconut, grated or 9 tbsps
desiccated coconut
8 green chillies
6 large cloves garlic
1 level tsp cumin seeds
2 level tsps sugar
1½ level tsps salt
2 tbsps lemon juice or white vinegar

☆ Clean, wash and cut pomfrets into 1½″ thick slices with bones. For other fish simply make fillets (without bones). Rub salt and lemon juice, keep aside for 30 minutes.
☆ Cut the banana leaves or foil into squares large enough to wrap each piece of fish. If you are using banana leaves then hold each piece over a flame for a few seconds to soften the leaf and the centre rib. Grease lightly one side of each leaf or foil.
☆ Grind together all the chutney ingredients to a fine paste.
☆ Coat both sides of each piece of fish liberally with the chutney mixture.
☆ Place a chutney coated piece of fish on the greased side of a banana leaf or foil and fold over. Seal the edges or tie with thread. Repeat the same with remaining pieces.
☆ Steam the fish pieces for 30 minutes, or place them in a deep dish with 6 tbsps of malt vinegar and cook on a low flame for 20 minutes or place the foil or leaf envelopes in a baking tray and bake (190°C-375°F- Gas Mark 5) for 25 minutes.
☆ Remove the threads before serving. Serve hot.

Note: "Patra-ni-Macchi" is a traditional dish served at 'Lagan-Nu-Bhonu' (Parsi wedding feast). When Parsis fled from their native Persia and arrived at distant shores of India they could not bring many things. Among them was their 'Cook Book'. But even though they could not bring those secret recipes with them like the Mughals, yet the created the exotic Parsi cuisine. A unique culinary art, which is an exotic hybrid combining something of both the land of its birth and the land of its adoption.

Cooking time: 45 minutes   To serve: 4-6

Lagan no Sas

Parsi fish cooked in spicy white sauce

2 (½ kg each) pomfrets or salmon, cut into fillets or steaks
3 medium onions, thinly sliced
5" green chillies, finely cut
3 green chillies, seeded and slit
3 cloves garlic, finely sliced
3 tbsps fresh coriander, finely chopped

½ tsp ground cumin
3 level tbsps plain flour
2½ level tsps salt
1½ tbsps vinegar and 1½ tbsps worcestershire sauce, mixed together in a bowl

¾ tbsp sugar
2 eggs, beaten
4 tbsps melted ghee or oil
9-10 cherry tomatoes, whole

* Mix flour with ½ cup cold water. Make a smooth paste, then pour 2 cups of water.
* Heat ghee or oil in a heavy based pan. Fry onions until soft but not brown. Add cumin , coriander, both the chillies and garlic. Stir and fry for 1-2 minutes. Pour in flour mixture and half the salt. Bring to a boil. Reduce heat and simmer over low heat for 15 minutes.
* Add fish pieces, remaining salt and tomatoes. Cover the lid and simmer again until the fish is cooked.
  Mix beaten eggs, sugar and vinegar mixture together.
* Allow the cooked fish to cool slightly. Add egg and vinegar mixture. Tilt the pan to allow the mixture to cover the fish evenly.
* Place the pan again over medium heat and cook further for 5 minutes before serving.
* Transfer carefully to a serving plate. Serve hot.

Note: 'Lagan no Sas' is also a traditional Parsi dish

Cooking time: 30 minutes   To serve: 4-6

Macher Jhal

A delicacy of Calcutta

½ kg salmon or cod (or any firm white fish)
8 dry Kashmiri chillies, broken into small pieces
1″ piece fresh ginger
2 level tsps cumin seeds, ground

2 bay leaves
8 whole peppercorns, ground
6 cloves garlic, crushed
2 level tsps black mustard seeds
1¾ level tsps turmeric powder
1 tsp panch phoran (see page 18)

1 level tsp salt
4 green chillies, slit
2 tbsps coriander leaves, finely chopped
Mustard oil for deep frying
2½ cups (575 ml) water

* Put ginger, dry chillies, cumin, peppercorns, garlic, ¾ tsp turmeric, mustard and 4 tbsps water in a blender and blend to a fine paste. Pour in remaining water. Mix thoroughly. Keep aside for 10 minutes.
* Strain the masala water through a fine nylon sieve. Keep the water and discard the residue.
* Clean, wash and cut fish into 2″ (5 cms) pieces. Rub little salt and 1 tsp turmeric powder on them.
* Heat mustard oil in a heavy based pan to a smoking point to remove the pungent smell. Fry the fish pieces few at a time until golden brown. Drain and keep aside.
* Heat 4 tbsps mustard oil in a separate pan over low heat. Add bay leaves and panch phoran. As soon as they begin to pop, slowly add masala water and salt. Increase heat, bring to a boil. Reduce heat, simmer until the sauce is reduced to half.
* Add fried fish pieces. Simmer again for 10 minutes. Add slit green chillies.
* Transfer to a serving dish. Serve hot. Garnish with coriander leaves.

Cooking time: 45 minutes   To serve: 4-6

Machhi Korma Qutub Shahi

Hyderabadi braised fish with aromatic spices, saffron, yoghurt & nuts

½ kg firm white fish
1 large onion, finely sliced
4 cloves garlic, finely sliced
1 tbsp fresh ginger, finely grated
4 dry Kashmiri chillies, seeded and soaked
25 gms almonds, blanched and chopped
1 tsp poppy seeds

1 level tsp ground cumin
1 level tsp ground coriander
1 level tsp garam masala (see page 19)
½ level tsp turmeric powder
2 tbsps lemon juice
½ level tsp ground pepper
4 eggs, hard boiled and halved

1 cup (250 ml) plain yoghurt
6 strands saffron
2 level tsps salt
2 tbsps fresh coriander, chopped
Ghee or oil
Hot water

- ☆ Wash and cut the fish into 2″ × 2″ (5 cms × 5 cms) pieces. Rub with salt, pepper and lemon juice.
- ☆ Heat 4 tbsps oil, shallow fry the fish pieces until pale golden.
- ☆ Put onion, garlic, ginger, almonds, poppy seeds and chillies in a blender or food processor with 4 tbsps water and grind to a smooth paste.
- ☆ Heat 3 tbsps oil in a heavy based pan, fry the ground spices until brown. Add turmeric and garam masala. Add 1-2 tbsps water if the masala begins to stick to the pan.
- ☆ Stir in yoghurt a little at a time. Stir frequently and fry until the oil begins to separate, pour in 2 cups of hot water. Bring to the boil, Reduce heat.
- ☆ Add fish pieces. Cover and simmer on low heat for 20 minutes.
- ☆ Pound saffron strands in mortar and pestle, add 2-3 tbsps hot water, make a paste and add to the gravy.
- ☆ Sprinkle coriander, cover and cook for 5 minutes more. Transfer to a serving dish. Decorate with halved eggs.

Cooking time: 45 minutes	To serve: 4-6

Saag Macchi

Spinach and fish with aromatic spices

2 (½ kg) pomfrets or cod, (or any firm white fish)
225 gms fresh spinach (or frozen), chopped
2 medium tomatoes, finely chopped
3 green chillies, seeded and sliced

3 cloves garlic, chopped
3 tbsps mint, finely chopped
3 tbsps grated fresh coconut or desiccated
½ tsp turmeric powder
1½ level tsps salt

1 level tsp white mustard seeds
Juice of one lime
4 tbsps sesame oil
Water

* Clean, wash and cut the fish into 2″ (5 cms) pieces.
* Heat oil and shallow fry fish until pale golden brown. Drain and keep aside.
* In the same oil put the garlic, chillies, mustard, coconut and turmeric. Fry for 1 minute and add spinach and mint, stir well. Reduce heat, add tomatoes and salt and cover the lid and simmer 10 minutes.
* Add the fish pieces, stir gently. Cover and cook until the fish is tender and excess water from spinach dries up.
* Remove from heat and sprinkle lemon juice. Transfer to a serving dish. Serve hot.

Cooking time: 30 minutes   To serve: 4-6

Tang-Ga

Assamese sweet and sour fish

½ kg salmon or cod
1 kg ripe tomatoes, blanched and chopped
2 medium potatoes, peeled and cut into thin strands
4 suriyamukhi chillies or any green chillies, seeded if desired and slit

Juice of one kagji lemon or other lemon (should be ½ cup juice)
4 tbsps coriander leaves, finely chopped
1½ level tsps sugar
3 bay leaves
1 level tsp aniseeds

3 level tsps salt
1½ level tsps turmeric powder
6 tbsps tomato sauce (optional)
6 tbsps mustard oil
Hot water

* Clean, wash and cut fish into 1″ × 2″ (2½ cms × 5 cms) pieces. Rub with 1 tsp salt and 1 tsp of turmeric. Keep aside.
* Heat 4 tbsps oil in a fry pan to smoking point, to remove the pungent smell and taste. Fry the fish pieces lightly a few at a time (do not brown). Turn gently or it will break. Drain and keep aside.
* Remove the seeds from the chopped tomatoes. Strain through a nylon sieve. Keep the juice.
* Heat remaining 2 tbsps oil in a heavy based pan. Put in the bay leaves and aniseeds. As they pop and splutter, add tomatoes and potatoes and chillies. Stir and fry until almost dry.
* Pour in the hot water. Bring to a boil, add remaining salt, turmeric and tomato sauce. Mix well. Reduce heat, cover the lid and simmer for 20 minutes.
* Add fish pieces gently with sugar and lemon juice. Cover again and simmer for 10 minutes until the sauce has thickened slightly. Add tomato sauce if you prefer a sweet taste.
* Add coriander leaves 2 minutes before removing from heat.

Variation:

Koni Engg Tang-ga — Proceed as above, using hard boiled eggs (make few gashes on each egg) instead of fish.

Note: 'Tang-ga' is a traditional Assamese fish dish. No Assamese lunch is completed without 'Tang-ga' during summer. Tang-ga was also one of the favourite dishes of the Assamese Ahom king, 'Chu-ka-Pha' also. Rulers like 'Kachari' (Bodo) and the 'Chu-Tia' and Mongkh Mair family also brought with them their own culture and recipes when they migrated from far East between 6 A.D. and 10 A.D.

Cooking time: 45 minutes   To serve: 4-6   Picture on page: 206

Lobia Aur Tamatar Salat

Black eyed bean and tomato salad

1 cup (160 gms) black eyed beans
6 medium ripe and firm tomatoes
1 medium onion, chopped
2 tbsps fresh coriander, finely chopped

1 tbsp fresh ginger, grated
2 tbsps lime juice
1½ level tsps salt
1 tsp chilli powder

2 green chillies, seeded and chopped
Juice of one lemon
2 cloves garlic, chopped (optional)

☆ Soak black eyed beans **overnight.** Next day boil until soft. Drain well and keep aside.
☆ Halve tomatoes and remove seeds.
☆ Place boiled beans and tomatoes in a large bowl. Add rest of ingredients. Toss well.
☆ Transfer into a glass serving bowl. Chill before serving.

Preparation time: 25 minutes   To serve: 4-6

Piaz aur Hare Aam ki Salat

Onion and green mango salad

2 medium onions, grated
1 medium green mango, peeled and grated

1 level tsp cumin seeds, 1 dry red chilli — dry roasted and powdered

2 level tsps granulated sugar
1 level tsp salt

☆ Squeeze out all water from grated mango. Add salt and keep aside.
☆ Mix together grated onion, mango, sugar, cumin and chilli. Chill and serve.

Preparation time: 10 minutes   To serve: 4-6

Adrak aur Tamatar Salat

Ginger and tomato salad

4 medium firm and ripe tomatoes
50 gms fresh ginger, sliced thinly
and salted

2 green chillies, sliced thinly
½ tsp salt
¼ tsp ground black pepper

4 tbsps lemon juice
1 tbsp fresh parsley or mint,
finely chopped

* Soak ginger and chillies in 2 tbsps lemon juice and dash of salt. Keep aside.
* Place sliced tomatoes in a serving dish sprinkle remaining salt, black pepper.
* Arrange sliced ginger and chillies on top and sprinkle remaining lemon juice. Chill before
  serving.
* Garnish with parsley or mint.

| Preparation time: 10 minutes | To serve: 4-6 | Picture on page: 154 |

Piaz Sambal

Onion sambal

2 medium onions, finely sliced
2 tbsps lemon juice

½ tsp chilli powder
½ tsp salt

Sprinkle onions with salt, chilli powder and lemon juice. Mix well and serve. This should
be made just before serving.

| Preparation time: 5 minutes | To serve: 4-6 |

Kosumbari

Traditional south Indian mixed salad

4 tbsps sprouted green gram
4 tbsps fresh coconut, grated
4 tbsps green mango, minced with peel

1 small carrot, scraped and minced
1 small cucumber, peeled, seeded and chopped finely
3 tbsps lemon juice

1½ level tsps salt
2 green chillies, seeded and sliced
1 tsp mustard seeds
1 tbsp oil

* Mix the sprouts, coconut, mango, carrot, cucumber, salt, chillies and lemon juice in a bowl.
* Heat oil, fry mustard seeds until they begin to pop. Add vegetable mixture. Stir well for a minute. Chill before serving.

Preparation time: 25 minutes   To serve: 4-6   Picture on page: 22?

Chaat

Indian fruit and vegetable salad

2 medium apples
1 pear, peeled
2 bananas
1 orange or sweet lime
1 small guava

½ cucumber, peeled
2 tomatoes
1 small sweet potato, boiled and peeled
1 medium potato, boiled and peeled

1 level tsp salt
½ level tsp chilli powder
1 level tbsp chaat masala (see page 18)
Juice of 2 lemons

* Cut the potato and sweet potato into bite size chunks.
* Peel orange and cut each segment into 2 or 3 pieces.
* Cut the apples, guava, pear, tomatoes, cucumber into bite size chunks. Sprinkle half the lemon juice.
* Slice bananas and toss in 2 tbsps lemon juice.
* Mix all the fruits, vegetables and spices together. Mix well. Cover and chill before serving.

Preparation time: 20 minutes   To serve: 4-6

Plain Raita

2 cups (500 ml) natural yoghurt
1 tsp cumin seeds, roasted and ground
1½ tsps salt

Dash of black pepper
1 tsp coriander leaves, finely chopped

Mix all ingredients together in a bowl. Keep in a cool place until required.

Note: Raita is indispensable accompaniment of Indian cuisine.

Preparation time: 2 minutes   To serve: 4-6

Boondi ka Raita

Traditional raita

recipe of plain raita
tsp sugar, optional
½ tsp mustard powder
1¼ cups (275 ml) cold water

For boondi
1 cup (100 gms) gram flour
Pinch of baking powder
Cold water
Oil for deep frying

For garnishing
1 green chilli, seeded and finely chopped
2 tbsps coriander leaves, chopped
1 tsp cumin seeds, roasted and ground

Sift gram flour and baking powder in a bowl. Gradually beat in enough cold water to make a thick batter.

Heat the oil in a deep frying pan. Pour a little of the batter on a ladle with holes and quickly shake the ladle over the hot oil so that small drops of the batter fall in the oil. Fry for 2-3 minutes until golden colour. Repeat with the remaining batter.

Drain the boondis on kitchen paper. Put all boondis into a bowl of cold water. Gently squeeze the boondis to remove most of the water.

Place boondis in a bowl. Add sugar, mustard powder and water to the plain raita. Add the raita to the boondis and mix gently. Garnish with chilli, cumin and coriander leaves. Chill before serving.

Preparation time: 25 minutes   To serve: 6-8   Picture on page: 67

217

Nawabi Raita

Grated carrots, walnuts and raisins in spicy yoghurt

2 medium carrots, scraped, washed and grated
3 tbsps (60 gms) raisins, cleaned and soaked
3 whole walnuts, shelled and skins removed

3 strands saffron, soaked in 1 tbsp hot water
2 level tsps salt
½ level tsp ground black pepper

1 level tsp chilli powder
2 tbsps fresh mint leaves, finely chopped
2 cups (500 ml) plain yoghurt
⅝ cup (150 ml) water

- ☆ Mix together yoghurt and water, add salt, black pepper, saffron solution, chilli powder. Churn well. Keep in a cool place.
- ☆ Break walnuts into small pieces.
- ☆ Add carrots, raisins and walnuts into the yoghurt mixture. Mix well.
- ☆ Pour into a glass serving bowl, chill, sprinkle chopped mint before serving.

Preparation time: 15 minutes   To serve: 4-6

Alu ka Raita

Potato raita

1 recipe plain raita
6 medium potatoes, boiled, peeled and diced
1 medium onion, chopped

½ tsp pepper
1 level tsp cumin seeds, roasted and ground
1 tsp sugar

1 tbsp finely chopped mint or coriander leaves
2 green chillies, seeded and cut finely (optional)

- ☆ Make plain raita as per instructions given on page 217.
- ☆ Add sugar and pepper, potatoes and onions. Mix well. Add chillies, if desired.
- ☆ Garnish with roasted cumin seeds and chopped mint.

Preparation time: 10 minutes   To serve: 6-8

Mixed Vegetable Raita

recipe plain raita (see page 217)
cup cauliflower, finely chopped
cup cucumber, peeled and
hopped
medium onion, finely chopped

6 cloves garlic, crushed
2 tomatoes, deseeded and chopped
2 tbsps coriander leaves, chopped
1 green chilli, deseeded and
chopped

2 medium potatoes, boiled
peeled and diced
½ tsp mustard powder
1 tsp cumin seeds, roasted
and ground

Combine all chopped ingredients except coriander leaves and cumin seeds.
Mix thoroughly and pour into a serving bowl. Sprinkle roasted ground cumin seeds and
chopped coriander leaves.
Chill before serving.

reparation time: 20 minutes   To serve: 6   Picture on page: 171

Piaz Tamatar ka Raita

Onion and tomato raita

medium onions, finely chopped
medium tomatoes, seeded and
hopped
cups (500 ml) plain yoghurt, lightly
eaten

⅝ cup (150 ml) water
1½ level tsps salt
Pinch of mustard powder
½ level tsp sugar (optional)

½ level tsp ground black
pepper
1 level tsp chilli powder
1 tbsp fresh coriander leaves,
finely chopped

Mix together yoghurt, water, salt, mustard, sugar, pepper and chilli powder.
Add onion and tomatoes. Stir well.
Serve garnished with coriander leaves.

reparation time: 10 minutes   To serve: 4-6

Baingan Pachadi

Egg plant in spicy yoghurt

1 medium egg plant, peeled and sliced
1 medium onion, chopped
1 medium tomato, chopped
1 green chilli, seeded and sliced

1 tsp chilli powder
1 tsp garam masala (see page 19)
1 tsp black mustard seeds
1 level tsp salt
4 tbsps water

2 tbsps fresh coriander leaves, finely chopped
2 cups (500 ml) yoghurt
5 tbsps oil

☆ Heat oil in a pan, fry mustard seeds, as they pop add onion and green chilli. Fry until onion is soft.
☆ Add egg plant, stir and fry for few minutes.
☆ Add tomato, chilli powder, salt and garam masala. Stir well and add water. Cover and cook until egg plant and tomato can be mashed to a puree. Cool.
☆ Add yoghurt and half the coriander leaves. Mix well. Chill.
☆ Sprinkle remaining coriander leaves before serving.

Cooking time: 5 minutes   To serve: 4-6

Bagaru Pudina ka Dahi

Mint flavoured yoghurt

2 cups (500 ml) yoghurt
200 gms fresh mint leaves
1 tsp mustard seeds
10 cloves

2" piece cinnamon, broken into 4
4 bay leaves
6 Kashmiri red chillies, each broken into 2

2 level tsps salt
6 peppercorns
3 tbsps ghee
6 large cardamoms

☆ Clean, wash and remove mint leaves from the stem.
☆ Heat ghee in a pan. Put bay leaves, peppercorns, cardamoms, cinnamons, cloves, red chillies, mustard seeds and salt. After a minute add mint leaves, stir and remove from heat.
☆ When cool, add yoghurt and mix lightly.

Preparation time: 5 minutes   To serve: 4-6   Picture on page: 12

Keley ka Raita

Banana sliced in spicy yoghurt and tamarind sauce

2 cups (500 ml) plain yoghurt
3 ripe but firm bananas
1 level tbsp cumin seeds, roasted
and ground

1 level tsp chilli powder
1 green chilli, seeded and sliced
thinly
8 tbsps imly chutney (see page 233)

* Whisk yoghurt lightly. Add all the seasonings except bananas and mix well. Chill.
* Peel and slice bananas into ¼" (1 cm) slices. Mix carefully. Chill before serving.

Preparation time: 15 minutes	To serve: 4-6

Phalon ka Raita

recipe plain raita (see page 217)
tsp cumin seeds, roasted and
ground
2 tbsps castor sugar (optional)
bananas, peeled and sliced

1 medium apple
50 gms seedless grapes
2 rings slices of pineapple, drained
and chopped

1 orange, finely chopped
1 small cucumber, skinned,
seeded and diced
Juice of 1 lime

* Core apple and chop finely with the peel. Now place together with sliced bananas in a
  bowl. Sprinkle lime juice. Toss well.
* Put all the ingredients in a large bowl and add sugar. Pour plain raita over it. Mix
  thoroughly. Add the apple and bananas.
* Sprinkle cumin powder on top. Chill before serving.

Preparation time: 15 minutes	To serve: 6

Kakri ka Raita

Cucumber raita

1 recipe plain raita	¼ tsp mustard powder	2 tbsps coriander leaves,
3 cups grated cucumber	¼ tsp red chilli powder	finely chopped
½ tsp sugar	¼ tsp cumin seeds, roasted and ground	

Make plain raita as directed. Add sugar and mustard.
Peel and grate cucumber. Squeeze out the water. Add to the curd mixture.
Pour into a deep bowl. Sprinkle chilli powder and cumin on top. Garnish with coriander leaves.

Preparation time: 10 minutes   To serve: 6-8

Kashmiri Dahi

Yoghurt Kashmiri style

2 cups (500 ml) yoghurt	2 walnuts, shelled and finely	8 strands of saffron, soaked
3 tbsps (60 gms) raisins, washed and patted dry	chopped	in 2 tbsps hot water
	1 tbsp castor sugar	

* Place yoghurt in a bowl and whip well with a wooden spoon.
* Add all the ingredients to the yoghurt. Chill before serving.

Preparation time: 5 minutes   To serve: 6-8

Facing Page
Clockwise:

Lucknowi Korma
Kosumbari and Achaar
Dahi Luchi
Malabar Narengi Ras
Banjara Roti

Chukkandar ka Raita

Beetroot in spicy yoghurt

2 medium beetroots, boiled, peeled and diced
1 tbsp ground cumin seeds, roasted
2 green chillies, seeded and chopped

4 tbsps fresh coriander leaves, finely chopped
1 level tsp salt
¼ tsp mustard powder

½ level tsp ground black pepper
2 cups (500 ml) plain yoghurt
10 tbsps water

☆ Whisk yoghurt in a bowl. Add water and whisk again. Stir in cumin, chillies, half the coriander, salt, mustard and black pepper. Mix well and chill.
☆ Add diced beetroot 10 minutes before serving. Mix gently so that both red and white colour can be seen on top. Garnish with remaining coriander.

Preparation time: 10 minutes	To serve: 4-6	Picture on page: 224

Khile-Hue Moong ka Raita

Sprouted green gram in spicy yoghurt

75 gms sprouted green gram
3 tbsps fresh ginger, finely grated
2 green chillies, seeded and sliced

1 medium onion, finely chopped
1 level tsp cumin seeds, roasted
½ tsp ground black pepper
1 level tsp salt

2 cups (500 ml) plain yoghurt
4 tbsps water
3 tbsps mint leaves, finely chopped

☆ Boil the sprouts for only 5 minutes. They should not break.
☆ Whisk yoghurt in a bowl. Add water and whisk again.
☆ Add all the ingredients. Mix well. Transfer into a glass bowl. Chill and serve.

Preparation time: 10 minutes	To serve: 4-6	Picture on page: 206

Facing Page
Clockwise:

Taihdar Roti
Chukkandar ka Raita
Sweet Warqi Roti
Hare Tamatar ki Chutney
Shorba-e-Anar

Palak Raita

Spinach in spicy yoghurt

225 gms spinach
2 cups (500 gms) plain yoghurt,
lightly beaten
1 level tsp black mustard seeds

1 level tsp cumin seeds
1 level tsp coriander seeds, ground
½ level tsp fenugreek seeds

½ tsp chilli powder
1 level tsp salt
2 tbsps oil

* Clean and wash spinach, discard any tough stems and steam over low heat until tender. Drain well and chop finely.
* Heat oil in a small pan, fry mustard seeds until they begin to pop. Add cumin, fenugreek and ground coriander. Stir and fry until fenugreek seeds are golden brown (do not burn).
* Remove from heat. Add chilli and salt. Cool slightly and stir in yoghurt. Mix well.
* Add spinach and mix thoroughly. Chill before serving. Sprinkle little chilli powder and coriander powder on top.

Preparation time: 20 minutes   To serve: 4-6

Dahi Nariyal Pachadi

Yoghurt and coconut pachadi

2 cups (500 ml) plain yoghurt
6 tbsps fresh coconut, grated
2 green chillies, seeded
1 tbsp fresh ginger, grated

1 level tsp salt
1 level tsp mustard
1 tbsp oil

1 medium tomato, cut
2 tsps coriander leaves,
chopped

* Grind coconut, ginger, chillies and salt together to a smooth paste. Add yoghurt and mix well. Add tomato pieces.
* Heat oil and fry mustard seeds until they pop. Pour over the yoghurt mixture. Stir well. Chill before serving. Garnish with coriander leaves.

Note: You can use grated cucumber (do not grind) instead of coconut

---

Preparation time: 15 minutes   To serve: 4-6

Tamatar ki Chutney

00 gms ripe tomatoes, blanched
nd chopped
medium onion, finely chopped
cloves garlic, sliced
tbsps fresh ginger, grated

1 level tsp chilli powder
1½ level tsps salt
1 cup (190 gms) sugar
8 tbsps vinegar
½ tsp fenugreek seeds

½ level tsp nigella seeds
(kalonji)
1 level tsp garam masala
2 tbsps oil

- Heat oil, put in the fenugreek and fry until light brown. Add nigella, onion, garlic and ginger. Stir and fry until golden brown.
- Add tomatoes, sugar, salt and chillies. Stirring frequently, cook over medium heat until the mixture has thickened.
- Add vinegar and garam masala. Stir and cook for another few minutes.
- Cool and bottle in an airtight jar.

Cooking time: 30 minutes   Picture on page: 172

Mangalorean Lassan Chutney

Garlic chutney Mangalorean style

6 cloves garlic
bedgi chillies (see page 24)
tbsps tamarind pulp

1 fresh coconut, grated
1½ tsps level salt

Grate the coconut.
Grind together coconut, chillies, salt, garlic and tamarind pulp. Sprinkle little water while grinding.

Note: This chutney should be served immediately. If you wish to bottle it, grind without water and store in an airtight jar.

Preparation time: 15 minutes

Nariyal ki Chutney

Coconut chutney

½ fresh coconut, grated
3 green chillies, chopped finely
3 tbsps lime juice
1 tsp salt

½ tsp split black gram, without skin
(urad dal)
½ tsp mustard seeds

3 tsps oil
½ tsp black cumin seeds
Few curry leaves

* Put grated coconut, lime juice and chopped chillies into an electric blender. Blend until smooth.
* Remove from the blender, scraping down sider of blender use little water if necessary and salt.
* Heat oil in a frying pan. Add urad dal, mustard, cumin seeds with curry leaves. Fry over low heat until urad dal is golden.
* Add the coconut mixture and mix well. Served usually with dosai and idlis.

Preparation time: 10 minutes

Picture on page: 11

Khubani ki Chutney

Dried apricots chutney

275 gms dried apricots, stoned
2 cups (280 gms) sugar
1¼ cups (275 ml) vinegar
4 tbsps fresh ginger, grated
8 cloves garlic, crushed

2 level tsps chilli powder
2 level tsps salt
2 tbsps (25 gms) almonds, blanched
and cut into slices

6 cardamoms, shelled and
crushed
6 dates, **soaked overnight**
and chopped

* Clean, wash and **soak apricots overnight.** Next day simmer in the same water until tender then grind or blend to a smooth consistency.
* Mix vinegar, sugar, ginger, garlic, chilli, salt, almonds and dates in a pan and heat slowly over medium heat until the sugar has dissolved. Stir and cook until syrup is made.
* Add apricots into the syrup and simmer for 10-15 minutes. Allow to thicken slightly. Sprinkle cardamoms.
* Cool and bottle in an airtight jar.

Cooking time: 1 hour

Picture on page: 6

Til Kopra Chutney

Sesame seed and coconut chutney

100 gms sesame seeds
1 cup (100 gms) fresh coconut
100 gms tamarind pods

4 green chillies
4 sprigs of coriander leaves, stalks discarded
1 medium onion, sliced

1½ level tsps salt
2 tbsps lemon juice

* Wash tamarind pods, add 4 cups of hot water, soak for 15 minutes and extract pulp. Repeat the same process to extract any remaining pulp.
* Grind together sesame seeds, coconut, chilli, onion, coriander and tamarind pulp to a smooth paste. Add salt and lemon juice. Keep in a cool place until required.

Preparation time: 30 minutes

Mango Chutney

450 gms green mango
2 cups (380 gms) sugar
3 tsps salt
2 tsps Kashmiri red chilli powder

½ tsp black pepper
2 tsps cumin seeds
½ tsp asafoetida

1″ piece ginger, chopped
⅝ cup (150 ml) vinegar
Little cold water

* Peel and shred the mangoes. Rub salt. Sprinkle little water. Cover and let it stand **for 5 hours.**
* Strain and squeeze out all water from mangoes.
* Heat vinegar and sugar together. Add chilli powder, pepper and ginger. Cook over low heat, stirring continuously until it becomes a thick syrup. Add mangoes. Mix well.
* Roast cumin seeds and asafoetida. Grind them together and add to the mango mixture. Cook until the chutney becomes thick.
* Cool and bottle it.

Cooking time: 30 minutes

Hare Tamatar ki Chutney

Green tomato chutney

225 gms green tomatoes
4 green chillies
1 tsp cumin seeds
4 tsps sesame seeds

4 tbsps grated fresh coconut or
desiccated coconut
½ tsp mustard seeds

1½ tsps salt
Pinch of asafoetida
6 tbsps oil

* Clean and chop tomatoes, remove seeds.
* Heat 5 tbsps oil and fry lightly sesame seeds, chillies, and coconut for 1 minute. Add tomatoes and fry for 5 minutes. Remove from heat, grind to a paste or put in a blender to make a fine paste. Pour into a glass bowl.
* Heat 1 tbsp oil and fry mustard seeds and cumin seeds till they splutter. Add the asafoetida.
* Pour it on the tomato paste and mix well.
* Chill before serving.

Cooking time: 10 minutes

Picture on page: 22

Dahi ki Chutney

Yoghurt chutney

2 cups (500 ml) yoghurt or curd cheese
½ cup green peas, boiled and mashed
2 green chillies

4 cloves garlic
1 medium size onion, finely chopped
2 tbsps lemon or lime juice
1 tsp cumin seeds, roasted and ground

1½ tsps salt
4 tbsps coriander leaves, finely chopped

* If you are using yoghurt then strain water from the yoghurt through a fine muslin and tie up loosely till it drips dry for about 30 minutes. Curd cheese can be made by hanging the yoghurt in a muslin **overnight.**
* Grind garlic and chillies.
* Place strained yoghurt in a bowl. Beat very lightly with a spoon. Gradually add all the ingredients and mix thoroughly.
* Chill before serving.

Preparation time: 35 minutes

Keley ki Chutney

Banana chutney

4 ripe bananas
75 gms tamarind pods
3 tbsps sugar
2-3 tbsps Kashmiri red chillies, dry roasted and powdered

2½ tbsps (50 gms) raisins
1 tsp cumin seeds, dry roasted and ground
1" piece root ginger, peeled and grated

2 tsps lemon juice
1 level tsp salt
2½ cups (575 ml) hot water

* Wash and soak tamarind pods in hot water for 15 minutes and extract the pulp.
* Place together tamarind pulp, raisins, sugar and chilli powder and stir well until the sugar dissolves.
* Peel and slice bananas. Sprinkle lemon juice on them.
* Add sliced bananas, cumin, ginger, and salt to the tamarind pulp. Mix well.
* Chill before serving.

Preparation time: 20 minutes

Seb ki Tikhi Chutney

1¼ kg apples
380 gms sugar
100 gms ginger, grated
2½ cups (575 ml) vinegar (preferably malt)

2 level tbsps chilli powder
1 level tbsp salt
10 cloves garlic, chopped
2 tsps cumin seeds, roasted and ground

2 tbsps lemon juice
3 medium onions, chopped
1 cup (250 ml) water

* Wash, peel, core and slice apples. Sprinkle lemon juice and toss well.
* Place apple slices, onion, garlic, ginger, chilli powder and water in a pan. Simmer over medium heat until soft.
* Add sugar, vinegar, salt and cumin. Stir well and cook until a thick sauce is made.
* Cool and bottle in airtight jars.

Cooking time: 45 minutes

Imly Chutney Mathurawale

Tamarind chutney Mathura style

1¼ cups (275 ml) thick tamarind pulp (see page 20)
250 gms jaggery, grated
1 level tsp black salt or rock salt

1¼ level tsp salt
1 tbsp cumin seeds, roasted and ground
1 tbsp fresh ginger, finely grated

1 green chilli, seeded and sliced
1 tsp chilli powder

★ Mix well tamarind juice and jaggery in a bowl. Stir well until jaggery dissolves completely.
★ Add rest of the ingredients. Mix well. Keep in refrigerator until required.

Preparation time: 15 minutes

Bamboo Shoot Chutney

1 (8″ to 12″ in length) fresh bamboo shoot
1 cup (190 gms) sugar

6 cardamoms, shelled and crushed,
½ level tsp nigella (kalonji),
1 (1″) piece cinnamon and 1 level tsp cumin seeds — tie them together

1 large onion, chopped
6 cloves garlic, chopped
2 level tsps chilli powder
2 level tsps salt
4 tbsps vinegar

★ Select a tender bamboo shoot, remove outer skins and soak in salt water **for 6 hours or overnight.** Change the water once.
★ Cut the bamboo shoot into 4-5 parts. Place bamboo shoots with enough water in a pan over high heat, changing the water 3 times, until tender.
★ Mince the boiled bamboo shoot pieces.
★ Place minced bamboo shoot, sugar, onion, garlic, chilli powder, salt with one cup of water in a pan. Stirring well, cook over low heat until the sugar has dissolved completely.
★ Tie all the spices in a fine cloth loosely and put it in the pan with the bamboo mixture, simmer until a thick syrup is formed.
★ Remove the spice bag and add vinegar. Cook for another few minutes. Cool and bottle in jars.

Cooking time: 30 minutes

Seb ki Mithi Chutney

900 gms cooking apples
2 tbsps lemon juice
1½ cups (285 gms) soft brown sugar
4 tbsps raisins

25 gms fresh ginger, grated
3 cloves garlic, chopped
½ tsp mustard seeds
1 tsp chilli powder

1 level tsp salt
2 cups (425 ml) vinegar
(preferably malt)

* Peel, core and slice apples. Sprinkle lemon juice and half the salt. Cover and keep aside.
* Place sugar and half the vinegar in a pan over low heat. Stir frequently until the sugar is dissolved. Increase heat and bring to a boil until a thick consistency is obtained. Cool slightly.
* Simmer apple slices in remaining vinegar until soft. Remove from heat and allow to cool. Stir in the sugar syrup with all remaining ingredients.
* Bottle in airtight glass jars. Allow to mature for 4-5 weeks before using.

Cooking time: 25 minutes

Pudina ki Chutney

50 gms fresh mint leaves, discard the stalks
small onion, sliced
green chillies

Juice of 1½ lime or
1 raw mango, peeled and chopped

1½ level tsps salt
1 level tsp sugar

Wash mint leaves and combine all ingredients in the container of an electric blender. Add 1 tbsp water. Run mixer at speed 1 for 30 seconds. Switch off. Push the chutney down with a rubber spatula.
Again run mixer at speed 3 for 1 minute.
Empty the paste into a glass bowl.

Variations:

Dahi-Pudina chutney — Add 2 tbsps of yoghurt to the chutney paste just before serving.

Lasan Pudina chutney — Add 4 cloves of garlic instead of onion while grinding.

Preparation time: 3 minutes

Achaar Mirch

Pickled green chillies with mustard sauce

½ kg green chillies, thick variety
5 tbsps mango powder
½ tsp turmeric
1 tbsp salt

3 tbsps mustard seeds, soaked
for 1 hour
1 tsp black cumin seeds, ground
1 onion, sliced

⅝ cup (150 ml) mustard oil
3 tbsps oil
Lime juice of 3 lemons

* Wash and pat dry the chillies. Make a slit lengthways on each. Remove seeds. Stuff a pinch of mango powder in each chilli.
* Drain mustard seeds, grind to a fine paste with onion and 1 green chilli. Add (150 ml) water and strain it. Keep the liquid aside.
* Heat oil. Saute chillies. Add strained mustard liquid, turmeric and salt. Cook 5 minutes until chillies are tender.
* Serve hot or cold with rotis or naans. Sprinkle lemon juice before serving.

Preparation time: 1½ hours

Chhundo

Grated Gujarati mango pickle

2 kg raw mangoes
3 tbsps salt
3 tsps turmeric

2 cups (380 gms) sugar
3 tbsps Kashmiri red chilli powder
3 tsps cumin seeds, roasted and
ground

* Wash, peel and grate the mangoes. Rub salt and turmeric to it well and set aside in a glass bowl for 1 hour.
* Squeeze out all water and add sugar.
* Cook over low heat. Stir constantly for 40-45 minutes until all water evaporates and sugar turns into syrup.
* Remove from fire and cool. Add red chilli powder and cumin seeds. Mix well and bottle it
* This pickle can be served immediately.

Cooking time: 2 hours

Lasan ka Achaar

Garlic pickle

25 gms garlic
Kashmiri red chillies
lemons

2½ cups (575 ml) mustard oil
2 tsps fenugreek seeds
2 tbsps salt

- Squeeze the juice out of the lemons and put in a jar.
- Peel garlic, wash and dry well and put into the lemon juice and salt, shake well and keep aside **for 4 days.**
- On the 4th day heat a little oil, fry the chillies and fenugreek seeds. Remove and grind them.
- Heat remaining oil. Cool and pour into the jar with ground chillies and fenugreek seeds. Shake the bottle well and seal. Ready for use after 4 days.

reparation time: 8 days

Kadukash

Sindhi mango pickle

kg green mangoes
50 gms salt
-3 tbsps Kashmiri red chilli powder
0 gms fenugreek seeds
0 gms aniseeds

2 tbsps black pepper, coarsely
ground
1 tsp turmeric
1 tbsp black cumin seeds
2 tbsps onion seeds

6 blades mace, ground
1 tsp nutmeg powder
4 sticks cinnamon
4 cups (1 litre) vinegar
4 cups (1 lt) oil

- Peel and grate mangoes or shred finely.
- Keep mace, vinegar, cinnamon and nutmeg separately.
- Add remaining ingredients to the grated mangoes. Mix well and put in a jar **overnight.**
- Next day coarsely grind mace and cinnamon and add it to the mango mixture with nutmeg and vinegar. Mix thoroughly. Cover with oil.
- Ready for use after a week.

reparation time: 8 days

Mixed Vegetable Pickle

Punjab

5 kg mixed vegetables (carrots, turnips, cauliflower, horse radish, etc.)
4 cups (1 litre) mustard oil
250 gms garlic

250 gms ginger
250 gms mustard seeds, 65 gms large cardamoms, shelled and
65 gms cinnamon — ground
250 gms salt

700 gms jaggery
5 tbsps Kashmiri red chilli powder
2 cups (425 ml) vinegar

* Cut vegetables into bite size pieces. Wash and place in a large vessel and pour boiling water over it for 15 minutes. Drain well and keep in sunlight for one day.
* Heat little oil and saute all vegetables for 2-3 minutes.
* Melt jaggery in warm vinegar.
* Grind garlic and ginger separately.
* Boil all remaining oil and remove from heat.
* Heat little oil and fry ground ginger and garlic, until brown. Add remaining oil with all dry masalas, chilli, salt and vinegar mixture.
* Cool it and add vegetable. It will be ready for use after 2-3 days.

Preparation time: 2-3 days

Aam ka Achaar

Hot mango pickle

2 kg green mangoes	5 tbsps mustard seeds, ground	2 tbsps turmeric powder
6 tbsps salt	5 tbsps Kashmiri red chilli powder	8 cups (2 lt) mustard oil

* Wash mangoes and wipe with a kitchen towel. Cut each mango with the peel into 8 pieces.
* Put all ingredients with ⅝ cup (150 ml) oil in a bowl and mix well.
* Place cut mangoes in a bowl with ¾ of the masala mixture and mix thoroughly.
* Put remaining masala into a jar with mango pieces over it. Seal well.
* On third day heat mustard oil till all smoke evaporates. Cool and pour into the jar. Mango pieces should be covered completely with oil. Cover the jar. It will be ready for use after 2-3 weeks.

Preparation time: 2-3 weeks

Hot Brinjal Pickle

Aubergine pickle

kg brinjals	1½ cups (275 ml) vinegar	2½ cups (575 ml) mustard oil,
tbsps Kashmiri red chilli powder,	1 tbsp pepper	heated and cooled
freshly ground	1 tbsp turmeric	4 level tbsps mustard seeds
6 cloves garlic	25 gms ginger	4 level tbsps salt
tbsp cumin seeds		

* Cut brinjals into cubes. Rub salt well and leave **for 12 hours.** Preferably in the sun.
* Grind together garlic, ginger, mustard and cumin seeds. Add vinegar and mix well.
* Squeeze out all salt water from the brinjals. Rub turmeric, chillies and pepper and add vinegar mixture.
  Pack in a jar and pour mustard oil over it. Cover and leave it in the sun light. Keep shaking, stirring it every day. It will be ready after 15 days.

Preparation time: 15 days

Gobi aur Mooli ka Achaar

Cauliflower and radish pickle (Punjab)

450 gms cauliflower
450 gms white radish or turnip
(shalgam)

3 tbsps black mustard seeds, dry
ground coarsely
2 tsps chilli powder

1 tsp ground turmeric
1¾ cups (275 ml) mustard oil
3 level tsps salt

* Peel and cut the radish into 1" (¾ cm) thick slices and cut the cauliflower into small flowerettes.
* Heat oil until smoking point and cool.
* Place the cut vegetables in a large bowl. Add salt, turmeric, chilli and ground mustard. Mix well.
* Add oil and mix again. Bottle in a large airtight jar for 6-8 days. Put the jar in the sunlight.
* Shake the jar 2-3 times a day.

Note: Green peas also can be added.

Preparation time: 8 days

Imly ka Achaar

Tamarind pickle (South)

250 gms tamarind pods, stoned
250 gms green chillies, chopped
roughly
250 gms garlic

250 gms ginger
1 cup (190 gms) sugar
25 gms cumin seeds, roasted
1 level tbsp turmeric powder

3 level tbsps salt
3 cups (750 ml) vinegar
⅝ cup (150 ml) oil

* Wash and soak tamarind in vinegar for 30 minutes. Extract the pulp and keep aside.
* Grind garlic, ginger, turmeric, cumin, salt and sugar in vinegar. Make a smooth paste.
* Heat oil and fry the ground paste for a few minutes. Add tamarind and chillies. Stirring constantly. Cook until mixture thickens.
* Cool and bottle in an airtight jar.

Cooking time: 40 minutes

Kandah ka Achaar

Onion pickle

kg small onions
2 tbsps salt
2 tbsps red chilli powder

1½ tbsps mustard seeds
4 cups (1 lt) mustard oil

* Peel onions with a sharp knife and make few slits in them. Soak them **overnight** in hot water.
* Grind mustard seeds.
* Drain water from the onions. Wipe them with a kitchen towel.
* Place onions in a large bowl. Add mustard powder, chilli, salt and oil. Mix well,
* Put the onion pickle in a jar and leave it in the sunlight for 2 days. It will be ready for use.

Preparation time: 2 days

Tamatar Kashundi

Tomato pickle in oil

kg firm ripe tomatoes, blanched
nd chopped
00 gms fresh ginger, roughly
hopped
0 green chillies, seeded and halved
engthways

1 large pod garlic, roughly chopped
1 cup (190 gms) sugar, 1¼ cups
(275 ml) vinegar (preferably malt)
— heat together
1¼ cups (275 ml) vegetable oil
1 level tbsp ground turmeric

3 level tbsps cumin seeds,
freshly ground
2 tbsps chilli powder
1½ tbsps mustard seeds,
cleaned and washed
1 tbsp salt

Soak mustard seeds in vinegar **overnight**. Next day grind to a paste along with ginger and garlic.

Heat oil in a large pan until smoking point. Cool slightly. Add cumin, ground turmeric, chilli powder. Stir and fry for a few seconds. Add tomatoes and chillies.

Pour in the vinegar mixture. Add salt. Reduce heat and simmer until oil begins to separate.

Cool and bottle in an airtight glass jar and allow to mature for a week.

Preparation time: 7 days

239

Nimbu ka Achaar

Lemon pickle

1 kg (about 35) lemons
250 gms black salt or rock salt

100 gms curum (ajwain)
100 gms black pepper powder

* Wash and dry lemons. Make 4 slits in each lime from bottom with a sharp knife. Make a sign of multiplication (X).
* Mix black salt, ajwain and black pepper together and stuff each with it.
* Put the lemons in a jar and cover the remaining salt mixture. Shake well. Seal well.
* It will be ready for use after 2-3 weeks.

Preparation time: 2 weeks

Shorsher Kashundi

Pickled hot mustard sauce

300 gms mustard seeds, cleaned
and soaked for 1 hour
20 dry red chillies, soaked in water
for 5 minutes

3 medium green mangoes
10 cloves
3 level tbsps salt

3 level tsps turmeric powder
Mustard oil
Hot water

* Cut the mangoes with the skin into thin slices lengthways.
* Grind chillies and mustard into a smooth paste.
* Mix together all the ingredients with the ground paste in a large bowl (or clay mutka), ad
  4 cups boiling water and stir well. Cover the bowl with a clean muslin cloth and tie it.
* Keep in the sunlight for **one full day**. Next day bottle the pickle in a jar, filling only ¾ of the jar. Pour enough mustard oil to cover the top, leaving an inch of space.
* Keep the jar in the sun for another 8-9 days to mature. Shake the jar once or twice a day

Preparation time: 8-9 days